LIVING BUILDING EDUCATION: The Evolution of Bertschi School's Science Wing

Copyright © 2014 by Ecotone Publishing
— an Imprint of International Living Future Institute

For more information write:

Ecotone Publishing
721 NW Ninth Avenue, Suite 195
Portland, OR 97209

Author: Chris Hellstern
Book Design: softfirm
Edited by: Fred McLennan

Library of Congress Control Number: 2014934824
Library of Congress Cataloging-in Publication Data

ISBN 978-0-9827749-2-2

1. ARCHITECTURE   2. ENVIRONMENT   3. PHILOSOPHY

First Edition

Printed in Canada on Reincarnation Matte paper — one hundred percent recycled content, processed chlorine free, using vegetable-based ink.

LIVING BUILDING EDUCATION

The Evolution of Bertschi School's Science Wing

LIVING BUILDING CHALLENGE

TABLE OF CONTENTS

FOREWORD

In the midst of unprecedented abundance, we are a people paradoxically haunted by the fear of scarcity and loss. Our economy, politics, and even education are largely driven by the unspoken fear of having less, but only rarely of being less. Fear is a primary driver of the growth economy, whatever our rationalizations and excuses. In its various guises, fear sells more guns, door locks, security cameras, trendy fashions, gadgetry to overcome social isolation, cars, and houses in gated communities. It also renders us voyeurs in the face of the seemingly inexorable numbers that describe ecological and planetary ruin and autistic to the needs of our descendants. Fear subverts the imagination necessary to design and build a world that works otherwise by charity, foresight, and forbearance.

I know of no answer to the paradox of fear that does not begin with improved education. But I do not mean the kind of education that teaches students to memorize lists of various things, to pass standardized exams, or to exploit an economy ruled by fear. Rather, we need the kind of education that cultivates ecological and moral imagination, refines the sense of beauty, preserves cultural memory, and hones the kind of intelligence that seeks out and honors connection starting with the people and places closest to us. It is the kind of education that engenders courage and permits failure for the right reasons. It is an education rooted in affection for the student and that nurtures the excitement that comes with the recognition that the world is still rich in possibilities. Its worth will be measured as service in the cause of life, not lifetime earnings. Such things are not easily taught in classes. More often they are absorbed by the students through the culture of the school, the dedication, competence, creativity, and kindness of teachers and, as we are learning, through the design of the school itself.

I first visited Bertschi School in November 2006 as administrators and teachers were beginning to discuss the design of a new building. That project was completed in 2007 at the U.S. Green Building Council's LEED Gold level. That remarkable achievement led to another: the design and construction of the science wing which is only the fourth building to meet the full requirements of the Living Building Challenge.

The story of the Bertschi School Science Wing is one of convergence. It began with the vision and leadership of Brigitte Bertschi, founder and Stan Richardson, director of campus planning, with the support of their board. The Restorative Design Collective provided the necessary design skill. The idea of The Living Building Challenge was articulated and developed by Jason F. McLennan, founder of the International Living Future Institute. The result is also a convergence, between education, design, and aesthetics that amplifies learning and creativity.

The students who attend Bertschi School are very fortunate to be in an innovative learning environment. They are taught by remarkable teachers in brilliantly designed and beautiful facilities. And they are mentored and nurtured in a school that is the physical manifestation of a world informed by charity, foresight, and forbearance, not fear.

DAVID W. ORR
Counselor to the President, Oberlin College;
Author of *Down to the Wire* and
Hope is an Imperative

ACKNOWLEDGEMENTS

LIVING BUILDING EDUCATION: THE EVOLUTION OF BERTSCHI SCHOOL'S SCIENCE WING

So many people made the Bertschi Living Building possible. From the students who dreamed some of the most salient educational features to the craftspeople who built them, this building was a true community effort. Throughout the project, numerous individuals readily donated their time, talent and resources to see this building constructed. I am grateful to Jason F. McLennan, Eden Brukman, and others at the International Living Future Institute for developing the concept and principles of the Living Building and continuing to nurture the cause of restorative buildings for our planet.

I sincerely appreciate Brigitte Bertschi, Stan Richardson and everyone at Bertschi School who were willing to take a leap of faith with our team in order to design and build this unique science wing to meet the demanding requirements of the Living Building Challenge and the School's own rigorous environmental and educational standards. Throughout the whole process Brigitte was always very welcoming, gracious and open to new ideas and Stan demonstrated great passion, patience, dedication and knowledge of every detail of this project. The Bertschi students were inspirational, eager to learn, and a joy to be around throughout the project. Bertschi School and its students made for a dream client.

I am thankful to have shared this project with my colleague, Stacy Smedley. We always seemed to be on the same page and on the same path with this project and we balanced each other nicely along the way. Stacy made it great fun. I also appreciate the willingness of KMD Architects to let us pursue this project and to lend us their support through completion. This project would not have been as successful or enjoyable without the complete dedication and pro bono professional expertise provided by the entire Restorative Design Collective. Inspired by everyone's unconditional willingness and excitement to be a part of the project team, each team member worked diligently to build the most environmentally and educational friendly building possible for Bertschi School and its students. I learned a great deal from each of these talented and committed team members.

Telling the Bertschi Living Building story has been a great joy that was made possible by Michael Berrisford at Ecotone Publishing. He was a pleasure to work with and pushed this project to fruition the entire way. I am grateful for the support of Mary Adam Thomas and her invaluable writing expertise that helped me to tell this story, and for Erin Gehle and Johanna Björk whose creativity and graphic design provided a brilliant visual experience for the book.

Finally, I extend a heartfelt thank you to my family who supported me throughout the Bertschi project from its inception to the last sentence in the story.

CHRIS HELLSTERN
2014

AUTHOR PROFILE

CHRIS HELLSTERN

M. ARCH. | NCARB | LEED° AP BD+C | LFA | CDT

Growing up with a deep affection for nature that was strengthened by his summer adventures in Alaska while serving as a Certified Level III Alaska Naturalist leading outback kayak trips, Chris has long been a passionate environmental advocate.

Chris holds a Masters of Architecture degree from Texas Tech University. His thesis work focused on designing a sustainable elementary school in Seattle that would allow both students and faculty to experience the building's many environmental features through education and practice.

Now with ZGF Architects in Seattle, Chris' professional experience spans a variety of project types including health care, justice, office, science laboratory, and higher education.

Chris has served as a Cascadia Green Building Council Branch member and a Living Building Ambassador for the International Living Future Institute. He also co-founded the Restorative Design Collective and the Seattle 2030 Roundtable, which works with local architects to achieve the 2030 Challenge. Since 2011, he has served as the first Regional Chair of Washington and Alaska for USGBC students. As a designer, co-project manager and construction contract administrator for the Bertschi project, Chris has been fortunate to travel around the country speaking at numerous professional conferences and universities. In addition, he volunteers with local school groups, mentoring elementary and secondary school students about sustainable practices.

Chris lives in Seattle with his family, spending weekends in the beautiful natural environment of the Pacific Northwest.

PART I

Context

The Ecology and Architecture of the
Pacific Northwest is home to Bertschi School

The campus sign that welcomes students each day

INTRODUCTION

On April 10, 2013, Bertschi School's Science Wing became the fourth commercial building in the world to achieve the most stringent sustainability standard for buildings, the Living Building Challenge, and the first to do so under version 2.0 of the Challenge. A few weeks later, during an All School Meeting on a warm and sunny spring day in Seattle, the International Living Future Institute (ILFI) presented the school with the award certifying that its new building had satisfied the Imperatives of all seven Petals of the Living Building Challenge after the required one year of occupancy.

Over 230 students along with parents, teachers, staff, designers and members of the community were present to take part in this momentous achievement for Washington State and the building industry. Overcoming often overwhelming challenges in materials, industry barriers, deadlines and budget, this Certification came at the end of an almost four-year journey.

The journey began with a single idea in late spring of 2009: to build the world's most sustainable school building that would offer a legacy of environmental education for generations. And when Jason F. McLennan, the creator of the Living Building Challenge, presented the award to the school and asked the students at the All School Meeting why

Brigitte Bertschi accepts the Living
Building Challenge plaque April 26, 2013

he was there, the children made it clear with their confident, simultaneous responses that they knew the exact importance of a Living Building. Nearly four years after the idea to build the Living Building Science Wing began, each of us from the design team listened as our hopes for future generations were affirmed. The students shouted responses of what makes their building sustainable to them. The students at Bertschi School understand the importance of their unique building and that is exactly what we all had hoped for.

The students at Bertschi School — and really anywhere — can teach us where we need to go from here. They inspire us to change and to do so creatively. They give us a reason to solve our environmental issues and guide us in thinking about ways to do it that we have never before considered. They give us a reason to make our planet a better place.

Sustainability conjures dreams of the future and how to protect it. Our children are the ones to live with the choices we all make now and they are the ones who can help solve environmental problems. The Native proverb that reminds us, "We do not inherit the earth from our ancestors; we borrow it from our children" drove the project team in part because Bertschi School is an honored institution that understands the concept. They teach children to be compassionate, confident and creative learners in a global community; a community they will protect and, all too soon, inherit.

Bertschi School's Living Building is not just a snapshot of one project in one city. This school and this building both have a higher calling: to lead by example and show us what architecture can be. They show us what architecture can do for our planet to advance education and environmental restoration.

9

The Pacific Northwest, also referred to as Cascadia, is a mostly coastal temperate region of the western United States stretching from Northern California to Southeast Alaska. It is one of the most ecologically diverse bioregions on the planet containing a variety of landscapes from rain forests to glaciated mountain peaks, oceans, rivers and desert plains. Near the center of Cascadia, encompassing most of the region is an area of about 10,000 square miles known as Puget Sound. Several major cities lie along the Sound but the largest is Seattle. Northwest naturalist Arthur R. Kruckeberg describes the varied geography of Puget Sound Country like this:

The Olympic and Cascade Mountains border the Sound with towering summits and countless ridges, slopes, and valleys. In turn, the mountainous terrain has created drainages of all sizes, from rivulets and creeks to great rivers. The lowland terrain has its own share of topographic variety: hills, valleys, streams and rivers, lakes, bogs, prairies, and forested flats and slopes. And where the land meets the pulsing tidal waters of the inland sea, still other landforms emerge: rocky headlands, steep bluffs, and wooded slopes. At water's edge come the deltas, estuaries, salt marshes, and beaches of rock, pebble and sand. There is diversity of landforms within and beneath the water of Puget Sound: bays, inlets, submarine canyons with sills and trenches and the mosaic of bottoms patterned by mud, silt, sand and rock. Surrounded by forest, Puget Sound, the long inland arm of the Pacific Ocean, reaches its way east through the Strait of Juan de Fuca and south down between the Cascades and Olympics. It is a life-support system of its own, yet it promotes response in its forest neighbors on all sides. The daily surge of the tides unceasingly restore the waters of the gigantic aquarium that is Puget Sound. Here is another living world, dramatically unlike that of the nearby forested land[1]

10

1   Kruckeberg, Arthur R. The Natural

Blakely and Orcas Island,
San Juan Islands, Washington

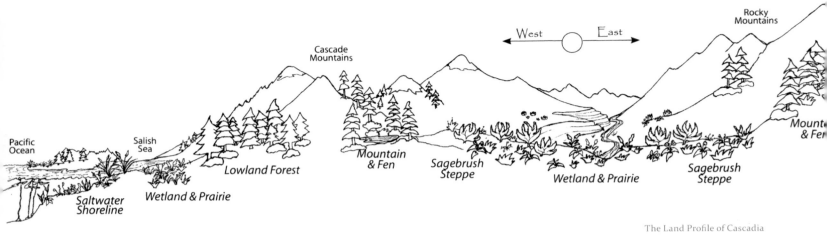

The Land Profile of Cascadia

From merely a description of the great geography riches of the region, one can see the complexity and beauty of the natural world that is so abundant in this part of the country. Nature is the predominant feature of the Northwest and has played a role in our daily lives since the first humans arrived here.

With a mild, temperate climate, it is one of the most beautiful places on earth, boasting an abundance of natural resources. The northwest enjoys mild, dry summers and temperate, wet winters along with rapid changes and localized weather conditions that are sometimes only separated by a few miles.[2] The weather in the Northwest is largely determined by the Pacific Ocean to the west and the surrounding mountain ranges. The ocean moderates air temperatures throughout the year and provides moisture while the mountains modify precipitation patterns and prevent infiltration of wintertime cold air from the continental interior.[3] While the precipitation amounts vary dramatically throughout the Northwest because of the differing terrain and ecosystems, rainfall is typically lighter than the eastern United States. However, the Northwest experiences a much greater amount of days with a trace amount of precipitation than the eastern part of the country. Seattle, for example has around 230 cloudy days compared to 160 in Boston.[4] The majority of precipitation here falls from November through February and the drier months occur from July through September. Although the weather in this region can generally be considered mild, the Pacific Northwest experiences some of the most severe weather on the continent. Strong winds, devastating floods and heavy snowstorms are known to plague the region.[5] With all of this natural beauty and constantly changing environment within such close proximity to Cascadia residents, the desire to protect it for future generations comes easily to those who live here.

2 Mass, Cliff. The Weather of The Pacific Northwest. University of Washington Press, Seattle, WA, 2008.
3 Ibid

4 Ibid
5 Ibid

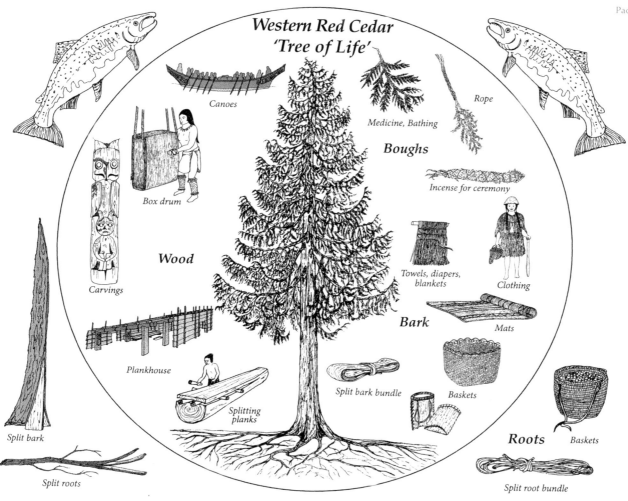

Western Red Cedar 'Tree of Life'

Canoes

Box drum

Carvings

Wood

Plankhouse

Splitting planks

Split bark

Split roots

Medicine, Bathing

Rope

Boughs

Incense for ceremony

Towels, diapers, blankets

Clothing

Bark

Mats

Split bark bundle

Baskets

Roots

Baskets

Split root bundle

PACIFIC NORTHWEST ARCHITECTURE

The architectural style of the Pacific Northwest has four distinct phases: Northwest Coast Native American, Early Regional Modernism beginning prior to and after World War II, Northwest Contemporary Style of the 1960s and 1970s and Northwest Regionalism from the 1990s to the present.[6] From the very first structures designed by the Native Peoples who inhabited the area, a response to the natural world has been essential. These Native Peoples built structures that responded to the climate and used local, natural materials out of necessity.

6   Miller, David E. Toward A New Regionalism: Environmental Architecture in the Pacific Northwest University of Washington Press, Seattle, WA, 2005.

Fleming Residence,
Paul Hayden Kirk 1953

Because the weather in the Cascadia region varies greatly from blustery winds at the coast to heavy snows in the mountains and plains, the native architecture also varied greatly. Some of the first people to inhabit Cascadia around 5,000 years ago lived in earth-sheltered homes. As the very first sustainable designers, the Cascadia Natives understood the importance of insulation, using mats made from cattail or tules to block winter winds and hold in heat from fire pits.[7] These homes eventually evolved into varied styles of above-grade structures depending on the particular climate response in their region.[8] Although not many of these actual structures exist today, the vernacular of deep overhangs to shelter from rain and cedar plank exteriors, for example, continue to be used today and are among some of the most predominant architectural characteristics of Pacific Northwest design. However, as technology developed and people began to rely more on mechanical means for heating and cooling, the tendency was to move away from basic design principles that effectively responded to climate. With this shift, we began to transition to buildings that were tied more to nature by needing to respond to its elements and the early lessons from the first people to live with the land were seemingly forgotten.

7   Ibid
8   Bohan, Heidi The People of Cascadia: Pacific Northwest Native American History 4 Culture, Seattle, WA 2009

14

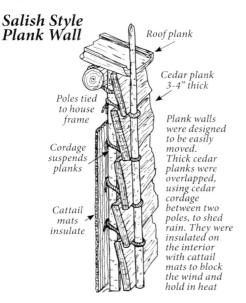

Salish Style Plank Wall

Bertschi's Living Building uses cedar siding design borrowed from the first peoples

Roof plank

Cedar plank 3-4" thick

Poles tied to house frame

Cordage suspends planks

Cattail mats insulate

Plank walls were designed to be easily moved. Thick cedar planks were overlapped, using cedar cordage between two poles, to shed rain. They were insulated on the interior with cattail mats to block the wind and hold in heat

Giovanelli Residence, Wendell Lovett 1959

During the Early Regional Modernism period, Pacific Northwest architecture had not defined a particular style of its own. Instead, much of the designs were characterized by the Beaux Arts period.[9] This style is classical with heavy ornamental features. Well-known examples of these designs can be found in the nation's Capitol such as the Library of Congress or the Jefferson Building.

Following World War II, a group of architects transformed the architectural style of the Northwest into their own reflection of the modernism movement that had taken over the rest of the world from architects like Le Corbusier.[10]

Out of this group of modernists a now well-known set of architects emerged to create the influential Northwest Contemporary Style. Architects like Paul Hayden Kirk, Wendell Lovett, Victor Steinbrueck and Roland Terry had developed designs that were strongly influenced by the landscape, open to natural light and tied directly to the earth.[11] After

the International Modernism movement around the world had shifted buildings away from a connection to nature, the Northwest Contemporary Style returned the importance of climate-responsive design to architecture. These changes helped to define the regionalism of the Pacific Northwest and carry this influential design around the globe.

Shed Style Plankhouse

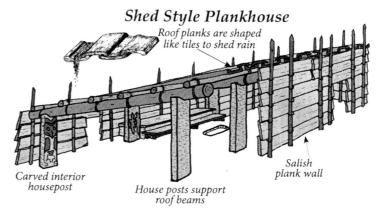

Roof planks are shaped like tiles to shed rain

Carved interior housepost

House posts support roof beams

Salish plank wall

Shed roofs are ideal for the pacific northwest climate

9 Miller, David E. Toward A New Regionalism: Environmental Architecture in the Pacific Northwest University of Washington Press, Seattle, WA, 2005.
10 Ibid.
11 Ibid

15

Lopez Island house with green roof, Roland Terry

Cedar plank walls designed by the people of Puget Sound

A BRIEF HISTORY OF SUSTAINABLE DESIGN IN THE PACIFIC NORTHWEST

Sustainability in Pacific Northwest architecture has long been a primary concern and these design responses are shown in the homes of the Native Cascadians. The climate here demands it. The first people required it. Even with abundant resources, the early people of Cascadia knew how to utilize their beautiful natural resources in the most efficient way possible.

The Western Red Cedar is a great example of how early civilizations used and respected natural resources to provide for nearly every aspect of daily life. The cedar, also referred to by some tribes as the "Tree of Life" (see page 13), was completely utilized when harvested. The branches were used for medicines or burned as incense. Bark was used to makes mats, baskets or blankets along with many other uses. Wood from the great cedar could be used for canoes, home building and ceremonial carvings while the natural oils were harvested to deter insects and decay. Even the strong roots were utilized

for baskets and rope.[12] The early Cascadia Natives were already practicing principles of sustainability to use their renewable resources wisely and completely.

Early Pacific Northwest architecture focused on fundamental design responses that make a significant impact not only on how efficient and contextual a structure can be, but also how it makes its occupants feel. Concepts such as proper siting (how a building is located on its site), building orientation, size and location of openings have always been carefully

12 Ibid

16

Kerr residence,
Pietro Belluschi 1944

considered in sustainable Northwest designs, helping to inform the local aesthetic. The mild-maritime climate of the Pacific Northwest lends itself perfectly for many design features that integrate well with nature. Natural ventilation performs well here, for example. And the long hours of daylight provide great opportunity to incorporate generous glazing to daylight and let in the spectacular, natural views.

A look back at some early designs from the Northwest Contemporary Style shows buildings that are beautifully integrated with their site, often set within the earth or deep in the forest. One of the first contemporary buildings in the West to incorporate a sod roof is located in Washington's San Juan Islands.[13] Simply following proper siting rules can be very advantageous for Northwest structures. They can benefit from passive solar heating, daylighting and natural ventilation. Our mild climate lends itself perfectly to passive and, consequently, sustainable design.

Some designs even touch lightly on the land, floating delicately on pillars above the varying topography of the Northwest. These buildings, with designs that are part of rather than separate from nature, have the power to evoke great emotions as they sit peacefully among their surroundings. But even with considerate designs, buildings are only ever just that. Pietro Belluschi, an Italian-born architect who practiced in Portland, Oregon in the mid-19th century, reminds us that, "A house can never be as beautiful as a tree."[14]

Koppel residence, Victor Steinbrueck

17

13 Ibid
14 Ibid

ARRIVING AT BERTSCHI CAMPUS

Bertschi School is a quiet campus that sits within an urban neighborhood of mostly residential homes. As one arrives at the school, it is difficult to tell where the homes end and the campus begins. This is a school that is truly part of the community, not just in aesthetics but in its mission.

Stretching out for a city block in Seattle's Capitol Hill neighborhood, the campus is bookended by two of its largest structures. On the south end of the block sits The Bertschi Center, the school's gymnasium, art and music rooms housed in Washington State's first LEED Gold-certified elementary school building. On the north end, rising high above the street, is an historic church building that has been transformed into classrooms. Between both structures are three historic single-family homes that have been converted into various classrooms and administration buildings. The entire campus has a scale that feels right-sized for the neighborhood — it fits among its surroundings and it fits among children.

The buildings consist of a variety of materials from plaster to brick to the classic cedar siding that is characteristic of Northwest architecture. Just like its home city of Seattle, the Bertschi campus is a mixture of architectural styles that combine to create a distinct block that relates to the community. From the busy street that fronts the campus, the laughter of children from pre-kindergarten through fifth grades can be heard rising above the traffic.

Sited on the far north end of Bertschi's block, attached to the converted church building, is the Living Building Science Wing. It is not immediately obvious to first-time visitors arriving from the more frequented south entrance, but when one arrives to the north end of campus, the unmistakable standing-seam metal butterfly roof is visible tucked beyond a healthy fence of urban agriculture. The building occupies a small site of only 3300 square feet, but it is densely surrounded by nature: green roofs, a lush garden with a variety of plants, trees, mosses and even insects and birds.

The Living Building clearly echoes the Northwest style used elsewhere on the campus, including in The Bertschi Center, the school's other recent project. The two buildings are meant to complement each other with similar cedar siding, metal and glass that pay tribute to the architectural regionalism and the structures of the Native Cascadia people. Although designed to be integrated into the campus aesthetic, the Living Building has something unique in its two main components: the tall, curving glass wall of the Ecohouse bursts out of the rectilinear cedar-clad classroom. This organically-shaped room is where the students investigate science through plant, soil, insect and other earth studies.

A SCHOOL IS BORN

In 1975, Swiss-born Brigitte Bertschi began teaching fifteen students in a leased classroom basement at a local Seattle elementary school focusing on what she believed to be the three components of a healthy school environment:

1. Understand how children learn best to reach them at their level and support them

2. Be part of a community of life-long learners

3. Encourage constant dialogue

With these values, she began to develop what would become one of the Northwest's premier private schools. Within a year, Brigitte had moved to a single building in what is now the school's current location in the Capitol Hill neighborhood. By 1980, the school had expanded to include first and second grade,

pre-kindergarten and kindergarten, each with two classrooms. In 1985, the school's first science lab opened to all 124 Bertschi School students. Two years later, the school acquired additional buildings in the same block to expand their education programs.

Since its founding, the school has continued to develop its campus to further its educational offerings to the community. Through each phase of development, the school has stayed true to its mission and values, first with an expansion made possible by adaptive reuse of historic neighboring homes, then with the first LEED Gold building at a Washington elementary school, and finally with its addition of the world's fourth Living Building.

Bertschi School occupies a city block in Seattle's Capitol Hill neighborhood. Their Living Building is at the far right.

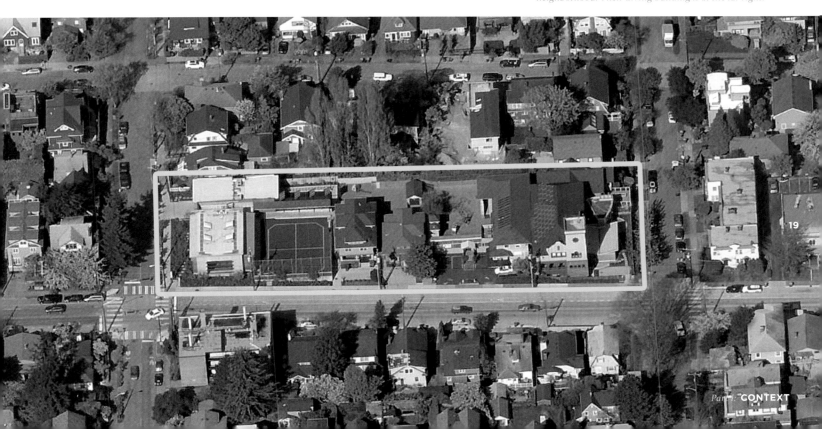

"With the integration of sustainable practices into our curriculum, our students are empowered to make a difference by learning, synthesizing, and sharing their newfound knowledge with our local and global community."

BRIGITTE BERTSCHI
Head of Bertschi School

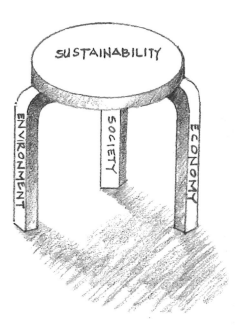

A SUSTAINABLE CURRICULUM

Bertschi's commitment to sustainability goes well beyond their facilities. For several decades, the school has been teaching sustainability values to its students — not just recycling, but holistic issues on a global scale. The sustainability curriculum at Bertschi is broad. Students study not only environmental stewardship but also diversity through cultural investigations and even economic lessons taking into account the three legs of the sustainability stool.

The concept of sustainability should not be thought of as merely singular. For something to be truly sustainable, it must consider environment, society and economy. Each depends on the other just as students depend on their teachers. Bertschi recognizes the critical role of young people in shaping a sustainable society. Educating students about sustainability begins with fostering a sense of wonder and caring for the natural world and its residents. Students develop these values through hands-on investigation both at school and in the local environment.

For Bertschi students, sustainability education is not just a week-long lesson about saving the planet offered on Earth Day. It is much deeper than that. Each grade level participates in a year-long investigation of concepts including energy, water, materials and waste. (Not surprisingly, these long-standing curriculum modules align perfectly with the Petals of the Living Building Challenge.) Their studies and inquiries are not limited to the classroom and the sustainable buildings on their campus. The students experience

nature in nature. They visit local wetlands, raise and release salmon and even travel to Islandwood, an outdoor learning center on Bainbridge Island.

On many visits to the school, I witnessed how the students take an interest in their sustainable topics and gain enough understanding to talk about them to large groups. I can recall one occasion at an All School Meeting where we were slated to speak to the students about their new Living Building. To our surprise, we were to follow a third grader who had just given a PowerPoint presentation about the school's waste stream. This student had begun this investigation on his own, approaching Brigitte to discuss his concern that students were not correctly using the recycle, compost and waste bins. He requested an audience with the school to discuss this matter at one of their All School Meetings. Prior to this meeting, he had done his own research and created a plan of corrective action for the waste stream issues. Later that year, he went on to present at other local schools, reporting on his findings and Bertschi's new waste reduction plans.

20

A SUSTAINABLE CAMPUS

Our children are shaped not only by the curriculum in their schools, but also by the buildings in which they study. Throughout its development, Bertschi School has always considered the right way to build. When the school first began to grow, it converted historic homes and an old church along Capitol Hill's 10th Avenue into classrooms. This is adaptive reuse at its best.

Director of Campus Planning (and Owner's Representative on the Living Building project) Stan Richardson recalls that in his first year at Bertschi in 1991, he was making a run to the campus dumpster at the end of the school year when he noticed nearly new materials had been discarded. He saw full sets of markers, a computer monitor, and paintbrushes which he recovered and his artist wife still uses today.

That is where it really started for Stan, pursuing conservation and reuse of school supplies and he helped to bring this awareness to the campus. Other faculty had their own initiatives to teach sustainability in curriculum through salmon and watershed programs. Together, these once separate pursuits converged over time to create a unified sustainability approach.

21

Around this time, Brigitte attended a National Association of Independent Schools conference and heard a lecture by environmentalist and professor David Orr. His words had a profound impact not only on Brigitte, but on other staff and school Board members as well, as she relayed her enthusiasm for Orr's ideas. These and other ideas, including those in the book "Cradle to Cradle" helped shape the instincts they had long held about conservation and transformed them into actionable policies for the school. Business leaders who serve on Bertschi's Board of Trustees were persuaded to change their attitudes towards sustainability, stepping away from merely a financial focus. This became a turning point in their thinking and inspired a shift in their awareness about sustainability.

When the school was able to make its first large expansion, it hired one of the most sustainable architecture firms in the country, Miller Hull in Seattle, to build what would become the first LEED Gold elementary school building in Washington State. Once again, Brigitte and Stan were inspired by David Orr and the Oberlin College campus to help clarify some of the ideas they hoped their building would demonstrate. While visiting Seattle for a lecture at the University of Washington, Orr visited Bertschi School and Brigitte and Stan had the opportunity to meet with him and discuss their ideas for the Bertschi Center Building. The building includes large cisterns for rainwater capture used to flush toilets and solar panels that are visible to students along with the use of many sustainable building materials. It was the school's first built venture into providing tangible examples of the sustainability they had long been teaching.

In planning to provide a dedicated science building, Bertschi School once again pursued the most sustainable solution, this time with a Living Building. The campus continues to improve its waste stream with an increasing percentage of recycle and compost rates. The students do not just track their waste, they figure out how to improve it through reduction. Bertschi not only teaches sustainability concepts, but also lives them. When they build their campus, they preserve their sustainable values.

Bertschi Center rainwater cisterns and PV panels

WHAT IS THE LIVING BUILDING CHALLENGE?

The Living Building Challenge is the most stringent sustainability standard in the world for the built environment. It is a philosophy, an advocacy tool, and certification program that encourages people to create holistic solutions for human habitat. It offers a compelling perspective for the building industry to change its processes to be more intentional and accountable. Launched in 2006 by architect Jason F. McLennan, the Challenge has developed into a globally recognized standard for true sustainable construction and operation.

McLennan gifted the standard to Cascadia Green Building Council, a chapter organization of the U.S. Green Building Council (USGBC), when he was named its CEO. With its great success and now global acceptance, the Challenge is now overseen and administered by the International Living Future Institute.

The idea of the Living Building Challenge is relatively simple. However, achieving it is anything but simple. It uses the metaphor of a flower, dividing the requirements (Site, Water, Energy, Health, Materials, Equity and Beauty) into seven Petals. But the flower metaphor does not end with the structure. It represents

24

Campus planner Stan Richardson,
Founder Brigitte Bertschi and Science Specialist
Julie Blystadt cut the ribbon on opening day

"*Living Building Challenge translates ambitious goals into tangible actions with measurable outcomes. It has been said that "sometimes the difference between success or failure depends on whether or not we get or give a little encouragement" (Richard Stine), and I believe that the Living Building Challenge does both — the program is a unique framework that not only describes restorative principles but it is also defined by the strength and support of its international community.*"

EDEN BRUKMAN
Co-author, Living Building Challenge

how the buildings should be; how buildings should perform. It serves as a guideline for restorative design rather than simply just green design. At this point in our global environmental crisis, when greenhouse gas emissions are at their highest recorded levels, when polar ice melt is at the greatest extent ever and the United States had its third hottest summer on record in 2012, the buildings we build right now should be helping to transform and restore our environment and not deplete it.[15]

A flower, of course, gathers all of its energy from the sunlight that strikes it. It grows with the rain that falls on it. A flower does not take away from its environment, but rather adds to it. Flowers and flora help to counter the list of climate change catalysts. That is the idea behind the Living Building Challenge — creating buildings that act like living organisms to restore our environment.

Because the built concepts of Living Buildings can be difficult to achieve, the standard is referred to as a Challenge, comprised of twenty Imperatives spread throughout the seven Petals. Two

15 EPA.gov

Part of the Restorative Design Collective gathers for the grand opening

simple rules help set the Living Building Challenge apart from other ratings systems (such as USGBC's LEED, which requires a building to go through a checklist of items that are projected to be met). The Challenge requires, or makes it "Imperative," that all twenty areas of performance are achieved. Not only must they be met once design is complete, but the building must also prove performance of all twenty Imperatives over a one-year period of occupancy.

THE TWO RULES ARE:

1. Achievement of all Imperatives are mandatory;

2. Living Building Challenge certification is based on actual, rather than modeled or anticipated performance.

Bertschi School and the Living Building design team elected to use the most current version of the Challenge at the time, version 2.0 which

was released in November 2009. When the team began the project, only version 1.3 was available. By the time version 2.0 was released, the team had already begun work with a schematic design submittal due in the next couple of weeks. But the team was eager to build under the most stringent sustainability standard in the world, and it elected to upgrade to 2.0. This version includes an expanded set of Imperatives over its predecessor. The Bertschi School Living Building is the first built project to attempt this version and to do so in an urban setting. Eden Brukman, co-author of the Living Building Challenge, worked with our team throughout the project, serving as the point of contact and mentor. Eden believes that, "because the twenty Imperatives of the Challenge are aspirational, it is not unusual for people to assume that they can only be achieved on certain building types or in limited circumstances. Bertschi dispelled the myth that a building couldn't be self-sufficient in an urban site."

25

Bertschi students review the floor plan of their new science wing

WHY DO THIS?

Many will say that the Living Building Challenge was developed out of necessity. We have to begin making choices that do not limit our future. There has long been a need for those of us with a passion for sustainability in the built environment to do more than something that is simply "less bad." There has long been a culture of buildings that are not improving our environment and in fact are helping to deplete it. Jason McLennan has developed a graphic to represent this idea.

At a time when even "green" buildings may still hurt our planet, we have a collective obligation to make real change in the built environment, which accounts for 40 percent of U.S. energy consumption alone. And while USGBC's LEED building standard is a great improvement over a traditional building that may not necessarily consider any sustainable designs that would reduce energy and water use, the Living Building Challenge is meant to create buildings that are restorative. Scientists, building professionals and many politicians have come to agree that we have reached a point where simply slowing down our environmental harm is not good enough. We need to be repairing.

Building a Living Building is not just about helping the environment in one dimension. The Challenge is distinct from many other standards because it addresses all three legs of the so-called sustainability stool (or triple bottom line): environment, society and economy. With Imperatives devoted to democracy, social justice and education, the Living Building Challenge factors in all three areas of the triple bottom line that are fundamental to creating truly sustainable systems.

Brigitte Bertschi has said that her school embarked on this challenge because it is "a learning institution. It was an incredible opportunity for us to take a risk and learn alongside our students."

"It's clear from Bertschi's history that the school cares a great deal about educating students completely so that they are getting both the technical as well as social and emotional pieces. I think with the environment that these kids are growing up in — with the challenges they have facing them and with climate change becoming more a part of their everyday world — it seemed like such a perfect fit because of what we were already doing with our curriculum. Their environment and how they live in their environment and treat their environment is going to be more and more an important part of their lives and they can't ignore it and we can't ignore it."

STAN RICHARDSON
Director of Campus Planning, Bertschi School

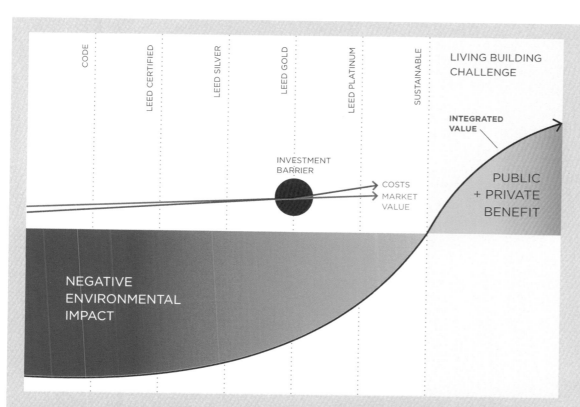

"Living Buildings are restorative and go beyond simply being 'less bad'"

JASON F. MCLENNAN
Author,
Living Building Challenge

As buildings move from "code" minimum standards toward built capital that is sustainable or even restorative, as with Living Buildings, their environmental and social impact begins to shift from burden borne solely by the public to that which benefits both private developers and the public as a whole.

Currently, an investment barrier exists around LEED-Gold thresholds when the costs incurred to achieve more sustainable buildings begins to outweigh their market value. By updating economic models to include the negative externalities associated with the built environment, an "integrated value" emerges.

A green building's integrated value includes its traditional market value in addition to the environmental and social value which it provides.

27

28

Ethnobotanical Rain Garden

PROVEN PERFORMANCE RATHER THAN ANTICIPATED OUTCOMES

Living Building Challenge 2.0 is comprised of seven performance areas, or 'Petals': Site, Water, Energy, Health, Materials, Equity and Beauty.

Petals are subdivided into a total of twenty Imperatives, each of which focuses on a specific sphere of influence. This compilation of Imperatives can be applied to almost every conceivable Typology, or project type, be it a building (both renovation of an existing structure or new construction), infrastructure, landscape or community development. Naturally, strategies to create Living Landscapes, Infrastructure, Renovations, Buildings or Neighborhoods will vary widely by occupancy, use, construction type and location — this is necessary — but the fundamental considerations remain the same.

PART II

*Inspiration to Pursue
the Challenge*

A Team Forms to Create a Living Legacy

Bertschi students hear about their upcoming Living Building at an all school meeting

Part II: **INSPIRATION TO PURSUE THE CHALLENGE**

CHRIS HELLSTERN

Growing up in Texas, I was exposed to a very different type of natural beauty than what I now experience as a Seattle resident. I was raised by parents who loved the outdoors and who made sure our weekend plans and most vacations included outdoor activities.

They encouraged me in Boy Scouts, serving in some capacity as troop leaders, and supported my journey to eventually become an Eagle Scout. And while each of these events helped teach me to embrace the outdoors, nothing did more for me than time spent in Alaska forming a personal connection to the outdoors and an appreciation for environmental education.

When I was twelve, my father took a summer job working as an Alaska Naturalist and lecturer aboard a cruise ship to fill his summer vacations away from teaching. Inspired by the unparalleled natural beauty of The Last Frontier, my family established a kayak tour business in the small Southeast Alaska town of Skagway. I spent the next ten summers there leading visitors on backcountry kayak tours, teaching them about the diversity, beauty, and importance of nature and our collective responsibility to protect it.

Those summer trips built a connection to the outdoors and an appreciation for education that has been very important for me. When it came time to go to college, I chose to study architecture back home in Texas. I think of architecture as the perfect blend of art and science, with the potential to protect nature. I had already learned that humans were causing harm to nature through building and development. And while I knew building would never stop, I felt I could join the profession to help our buildings be less harmful. I took this charge into graduate school and further investigated sustainability. My master's thesis focused on designing an environmentally sustainable elementary school in Seattle where the students were part of the building's many environmental features because I believe that environmental appreciation can be much more effective when introduced during early childhood. In 2005, that type of architecture seemed like the distant future. I hoped that by the end of my career I would be able to work on a high caliber project such as the Bertschi Living Building — a building that gives back to its environment by teaching its occupants about environmental conservation.

Immediately after graduating in mid-2006, I moved to Seattle to begin a career with KMD Architects. At KMD I was given opportunities to pursue my passion for sustainable design. A short time later, the Bertschi Living Building would become the embodiment of the dream for buildings that I once explored with my thesis.

STACY SMEDLEY

Stacy's journey to become an architect and to have a sustainability-focused career began when she was a young girl. It was born of her mother's inspiration and supportive parenting and the experience she had at eight years of age when she lost the natural world she had grown to love.

At that age, when standing on the deck of her house just outside Portland, Oregon, she recalls watching the trees surrounding her home and neighborhood being felled to make way for asphalt pavement and empty dirt lots for future home development. Stacy even remembers the smell of the newly-cut trees as she watched the trees she would climb and sit under to read were mowed down. This was the moment when she made a promise to her mother to create buildings that would not require any trees to be cut down. And while many youngsters would have let this promise go long ago, Stacy continues to honor her commitment.

Today, Stacy talks a lot about the future she hopes for young children. It is clear that her experience growing up has played a tremendous role in shaping what she does today. She wants children to grow up with the opportunity to remember a promise they made from a life-shaping experience. But she wants it to be whispers of hope and confirmation that the experiences they had in spaces like the Bertschi School were inspiring and impactful enough to instill within them the desire to care for their environment. She wants the trend to shift from negative experiences creating impact to positive spaces creating change. For Stacy, the Bertschi project was only the beginning — a first step down the path of providing children everywhere the opportunity to experience hands-on learning in restorative environments.

Stacy and her grandfather share
a book at her Oregon home

33

"I was immediately drawn in by the honest and passionate approach he (Jason F. McLennan) took with his presentation because he pushed us to talk honestly about the state of the environment and not hide from the seriousness of the problem."

STACY SMEDLEY
Designer, Co-Project Manager

LIVING FUTURE 2009

After nearly three years working at KMD, I began to try to find ways to increase my involvement with true sustainability work beyond promoting LEED projects. While my thesis work had focused on sustainability, I had been looking for a way to integrate this type of work in my career and become involved in this emerging portion of the industry.

I quickly found Cascadia Region Green Building Council. This non-profit organization is a chapter of the U.S. Green Building Council and the Canada Green Building Council, with a network of fifteen branches from Oregon to Alaska along with British Columbia. This organization is a leading advocate for progressive green building laws, regulations and incentives. Cascadia is a program of the International Living Future Institute (ILFI) and it works to set the global vision for the transformation toward true sustainability. It was in this organization that I found the sustainability work I was looking for.

The major event that ILFI organizes each year is the Living Future unConference that attracts the green movement's leading proponents and practitioners to advance sustainability. I decided to propose to my firm that Stacy and I attend the conference along with representatives of each of KMD's offices.

In the spring of 2009, KMD Architects sent its first group of delegates to the third annual Living Future unConference in Portland, Oregon. During research for my master's thesis in 2006, I had been exposed to the Living Building Challenge concept but at that time there was really no data — just the mention of a new standard for the built environment. But, at the 2009 Living Future unConference, we learned more about the Challenge and heard Jason F. McLennan's call to be change agents that would help make these types of buildings the new reality.

The conference was transformative for Stacy and me. This was the first time that I heard so many of the ideas that I had been hoping to practice in architecture. But this time, there was a path to help guide these ideas. I will always remember that year's keynote from biologist and author Janine Benyus about her life's work in Biomimicry and being captivated by her illustrative descriptions as she outlined many ways that nature has informed human advancements. Biomimicry is the science of studying innovative methods that seek sustainable solutions by emulating nature's time-tested patterns and strategies.

The following morning, Cascadia's CEO Jason F. McLennan spoke to the conference attendees. He began to make the case for Living Buildings and showed how they can create lasting environmental improvements. During Jason's plenary, Stacy and I excitedly made notes about moving KMD into this realm of sustainability. We realized we needed to push an upcoming project to take on the Challenge or try to find a willing client who was already interested. When Stacy and I returned to Seattle from this inspiring three-day gathering, we knew we needed to build a Living Building; however, finding a client who was willing to take on the Challenge we knew would be, well... a challenge.

To promote restorative buildings and make significant change with our work, we wanted to do something more than just create another research study or white paper. We wanted to build an actual building that would teach us as we designed it and teach others for years to come. It was not about building something merely adequate that we knew we could achieve but rather about what we might achieve if we pushed the limits of design. We believed that it was time for a built case study to serve as an example to show that restorative buildings are possible. Even with architectural or consulting firms that are aggressively pursuing sustainability, there is a disconnect between research and practice. Oftentimes the effort that is given to research does not translate into manifestation in the built environment. This failure of our industry can be due to the fast-paced schedule of projects or a particular client's willingness to implement sustainability. Of course, there is also the fallback of doing what we have done before. The Bertschi project needed to overcome these current shortcomings to be successful in pushing the boundaries of architectural sustainability. We welcomed the opportunity for the many challenges this project would present so that we could learn how to overcome them, not work around them. Soon we would find out that there were other people who felt the same way.

"When Chris and I got back from Living Future and had our first discussions about how to make the idea of a Living Building a reality, a lot of it was around finding the right project, and the right client."

STACY SMEDLEY
Designer,
Co-Project Manager

35

THE FIRST BERTSCHI TOUR

Only a few days after returning from Living Future, I was researching a dashboard for another project at KMD. A dashboard is a computer touch screen that is displayed in a building to showcase its environmental features. It shows a building's energy generation from a PV system, the rainwater that has been collected in its cisterns or any combination of data that represents the sustainable features of a project. The idea is that building occupants and visitors can see how their building is performing in real time. We wanted to see one of these dashboards in person before recommending it to another client and found that the closest one to visit was at Bertschi School, only a few miles from our KMD office.

I set up a tour to see Bertschi School's newest addition, the Bertschi Center, and asked Stacy and another coworker to come along. As the first LEED Gold elementary school building in Washington State, the building has a host of great environmental features. On the tour, we noticed the school had something special in both its facilities and its staff. We met Stan Richardson, who had a clear understanding and passion for the environmental features and sustainability value of the Bertschi Center. Stan has worked at Bertschi for more than twenty years and has a dynamic range of experience that includes a degree in industrial electronics and instrumentation and a degree in photography. Before arriving at Bertschi, his work as an inspector for Underwriters Laboratory (UL) and prior facilities and construction management experience keyed into his attention to detail and technical problem solving , which would prove invaluable to the Living Building project.

Having led many of these tours since the building opened, Stan was no longer participating in every one of them. Tour responsibilities were typically shared among other staff and teachers, but, because he noticed a group of architects was to visit, Stan decided to lead the tour so he could discuss more of the project's technical details. He walked us through the Center, explaining the school's commitment to sustainability and showing us the various building features.

As Stacy and I were concluding the tour with Stan, we asked if he had other building projects on the horizon. (He told us later that he thought we were fishing for work.) Stan mentioned Bertschi School's goal to construct a new science wing within a couple of years. What he added to that statement was the most important piece. He talked about the dream that this building could be built to a new standard he and the school's facilities committee had just heard about: a Living Building.

Although Stan recalls our reaction upon hearing about their Living Building dreams as "surprisingly subdued," Stacy and I remember being very enthusiastic — but probably just internally. We returned to the office thrilled. We talked about the possibility that the Living Building project we had hoped for just days before could now become a reality. We were pleasantly surprised to hear that someone outside the design-build industry had heard of the Living Building Challenge. When Stan mentioned the science wing to us, he said there were no real plans for building yet and that their timeline for undertaking this project was probably still a few years away. Stacy and I knew it would be difficult to acquire a project that had not even been formally organized yet. We quickly came to the conclusion that in order to do this project, we would need to offer our services pro bono.

36

The Bertschi Center Green TouchScreen that brought Chris and Stacy to the school

Some members of the Restorative Design Collective at the groundbreaking site

GATHERING THE TEAM

Back at the office, we immediately began putting together a list of design team members we knew might be interested in a Living Building. We focused on past project teammates who we knew shared our passion for sustainability. On the same day of the tour, we reached out to these contacts with a simple request. We explained our experience at the Living Future unConference, about the school and about our desire to build a true case study to show that Living Buildings are possible and necessary. Our goal was to create Living Building expertise so we could develop a local team whose members would know what it takes to make one a reality.

We were surprised by the prompt and positive responses. What was so remarkable was the simplicity and enthusiasm we saw in the replies. After proposing this project through a lengthy email asking for pro bono services, we received many one-word or one-sentence responses: "Yes," or "I would love to be involved." The simplicity of these replies would continue to serve as evidence of each team member's true passion for sustainability and education throughout the project. Rae Anne Rushing, founder of our MEP Engineering firm, Rushing, was immediately interested in the project because firm members "pride themselves on their ability to adapt to design challenges that are outside of the traditional MEP 'core.'"

"When Chris and Stacy came to KMD with a proposal for this project at Bertschi School, it seemed like a good opportunity for both a rewarding project and advancing our experience in sustainable design in the community as well as a big step in the professional development of Chris and Stacy."

CHRIS GRIFFES
Director, KMD Architects

After Stacy and I assembled the team, we then brought the idea of a pro bono Living Building project to our firm. "We were operating on the inspiration that had overtaken us at Living Future and the impetus that this was something that we simply had to do," remembers Stacy. "It was only after we had commitments from the entire design team and contractor that we approached KMD with the proposal." We wanted to make sure that we would have the support of a design team before approaching our firm and, as Stacy points out, "there's something to be shared in the path that we took, that sometimes it is okay to act on passion that inspires a vision."

At KMD Architects, there has been a commitment to sustainability and working on projects that are socially responsible since the firm's founding fifty years ago. But perhaps more significant for pursuing a pro bono built case study like this one is KMD's culture of curiosity and inquiry. It is a culture that supports its employees and helps to grow their personal and professional passions. This culture was invaluable as Stacy and I brought the idea to the firm's leadership team, including our Director, architect Chris Griffes. They were excited about the possibilities but Chris remembers wondering how "this small pro bono project would fit into the business model of KMD." Despite this project being a risk that was completely outside of the firm's business model, KMD leaders immediately gave their support to initiate the project just as our consultants' companies had done. Similarly, when Mark Sindell approached his partners at GGLO, he notes that, "rarely have I seen such unified dedication in an effort like this – full commitment without hesitation from our firm and the project team."

Having compiled a team of experts in sustainable building located from Seattle to Bellingham, Washington, we decided that the team would need a unique name to identify that we were more than just a standard group of consultants. We wanted to convey our group's focus to build something more than just a green building – something that involved truly restorative architecture. The motive for the team was to build a living legacy that would educate and inspire generations of students and building professionals. It was in that spirit that we formed the Restorative Design Collective.

THE RESTORATIVE DESIGN COLLECTIVE

GEOTECHNICAL: GEOENGINEERS

CIVIL: 2020 ENGINEERING

LANDSCAPE: GGLO

STRUCTURAL: QUANTUM CONSULTING ENGINEERS

ARCHITECTURAL: KMD ARCHITECTS

MECHANICAL/ELECTRICAL/ PLUMBING ENGINEER: RUSHING

SUSTAINABILITY CONSULTANT: O'BRIEN & COMPANY

CONTRACTOR: SKANSKA USA BUILDING, INC.

URBAN ECOLOGIST: BACK TO NATURE DESIGN, LLC

BUILDING ENVELOPE ENGINEER: MORRISON HERSHFIELD

PUBLIC RELATIONS: PARSONS PR

The Restorative Design Collective was comprised of eleven companies that provided their expertise and passion for sustainable design completely pro bono for the Bertschi Living Building project. Each of these consultants worked through the completion of the project culminating in Living Building Certification in April 2013.

"The idea of striving to meet the most stringent sustainable design guidelines out there — something that, at the time, had never been done — in an educational environment that could change the thinking of children who will become our future leaders, workforce, and decision makers, was simply too good to pass up."

MARK SINDELL
Landscape Architect, GGLO

LIVING BUILDING EDUCATION

PRESENTING THE OFFER

Only a little more than a month after returning from the 2009 Living Future unConference in Portland, the newly formed Restorative Design Collective offered Bertschi School the opportunity to build a Living Building with no design fees.

Stan met with Stacy and me a couple of times to discuss details before he presented the idea to Brigitte and some of the facilities committee members. That group quickly brought the idea to the Bertschi Board chair and it was agreed that the full Board needed to meet to discuss this offer and the escalation of the school's master plan construction timeframe.

School was in summer recess at that time, so the Bertschi Board gathered for an unscheduled meeting to consider the offer on, as Brigitte so clearly remembers it, "a very hot, beautiful summer day." These are the days that make the cloudy Seattle winters worth it for many people; spectacular, clear days when snow-capped mountains are visible in every direction from the city. The sky and water are so blue and provide a brilliant contrast against the green trees. For many, this weather is the key element of Cascadia's natural beauty and what makes the region a hub of environmental stewardship. The setting was perfect for discussing a building that would attempt to celebrate and nurture its natural surroundings.

Once the Board had convened for its special session, Stacy and I were called to introduce ourselves and our concept. We both were feeling a mixture of emotions for this meeting and Stacy remembers them all. "I remember how excited and nervous I was and how hard it was to believe that we were so close to being able to start down the path of creating a Living Building. I remember being so humbled and I remember feeling proud to be sitting in front of the Board with such an amazing group of professionals." At this point, the school had recently completed the Bertschi Center and was not eager to undertake another construction project so soon. The Board did not yet have the funding for it. But Stacy and I, together with other members of the Collective, made our case for the shorter timeline in order to build the first Living Building on the west coast. At this time there was no other Living Building certified, although some were in design or construction phases. We wanted to show that a Living Building could be built and that we could create a team of experts who could accomplish it and present everything at the following year's Living Future unConference. As Brigitte discussed the opportunity with her Board, she recalls that the discussion that day had been positive and optimistic.

The Board unanimously voted to accept our proposal and undertake the Challenge. The driving force behind the Board's conclusion was why they should pursue the Living Building Challenge rather than why they should not. Bertschi School Board Chair, Mary Pembroke Perlin, recalls three key factors in their initial decision to pursue the Living Building Challenge:

First, the value of sustainability was broadly embraced across the leadership platform: the Head of School, the Director of Campus Planning and the past, current and future Board Presidents David Thyer, Udo Reich and myself.

Second, the Bertschi Board is deeply committed to the values and mission of the school. The Board was willing to embrace the risks inherent in the Challenge in order to see this unique manifestation of Bertschi's values.

Third, and very compelling was enthusiasm and commitment of the architects and the Design Collective. I like to joke that they had us at 'Pro Bono,' and while that was indeed a motivating factor, what truly drove this decision forward was the depth and strength of the commitment by this group of professionals.

BUILDING BERTSCHI'S VALUES

We are often asked: Why do this? Why would a school undertake a building challenge seemingly unrelated to education?

These are signficant questions that Mary Pembroke Perlin and other Board members pondered and kept coming back to the simple answer that, "sustainability is a clearly articulated value at Bertschi and a Living Building was the perfect opportunity to demonstrate and truly realize the school's commitment to sustainable practices." Simply teaching sustainability is not enough for the school because the leaders and teachers recognize that the place where students learn also matters. It matters how healthy their indoor air is. It matters how much daylight they have to improve their performance. It matters what they can teach the next generation of students. At Bertschi, they continually strive to practice what they

teach. They construct buildings that embody the values of sustainability in conservation and restoration concepts they teach their students.

Childhood experiences can plant important values that last a lifetime. While there have been many influences in sustainability throughout her career, Brigitte recalls some from her home in Switzerland. There, she was familiar with a different focus for buildings — consideration of basic environmental principles and energy efficiency. She compares the thick walls of Swiss buildings to the thin wall buildings that are often built in America. So often, she feels, basic building standards in America are not focused on sustainability but instead on a more short-term interest.

41

DESIGNING A LIVING BUILDING: STUDENT COLLABORATION

As architects, it is sometimes easy to focus on buildings alone. Architects talk about the shape of their buildings and what it means. They talk about the materials used, the project cost, the challenges or what the best angle might be that offers the best view of the structure. Even with ultra-sustainable buildings, it is possible to get caught up in the details of the systems, becoming engrossed in energy use numbers, water savings, the unique system that makes the building stand out or how much recycled content was used.

But architecture and sustainability are more than systems and numbers. They are first about people and nature, and that principle is encouraged by the Living Building Challenge.

Perhaps this principle is no more important than when applied in an educational setting. And when it came time to design a building for students, team members thought about how children will be the key to solving our sustainability issues. The team wanted to hear directly from them and be inspired by their unfiltered creativity, so we asked Julie Blystad, Bertschi School's science specialist, to talk with her students. She returned to us with an astonishing wish list of items from her students. "They have many more ideas," Julie said. "But we ran out of time and I didn't change their language." The students truly created their wish list.

What is great about working with students is that they are not restricted by the same boundaries on ideas that often confine adults. They think about what they want and not what society convinces us might be possible. They simply think like children and they helped the Restorative Design Collective to do the same.

Some of the student's exact wishes that the team incorporated in the design were:

- Three-foot square floor tiles made of glass. Maybe a stream could be running under the classroom. The floor tiles would be removable so there could be water testing.

- A bamboo type fountain where students could go and sit to relieve their stress. (Frank Lloyd Wright's "Falling Water" was mentioned.)

- Cisterns to collect water that are clear so the students could see and monitor the rainfall.

- A greenhouse where something would be always growing.

- Could the outside fence have vegetables growing on it?

Students writing their Living Building design wish list

42

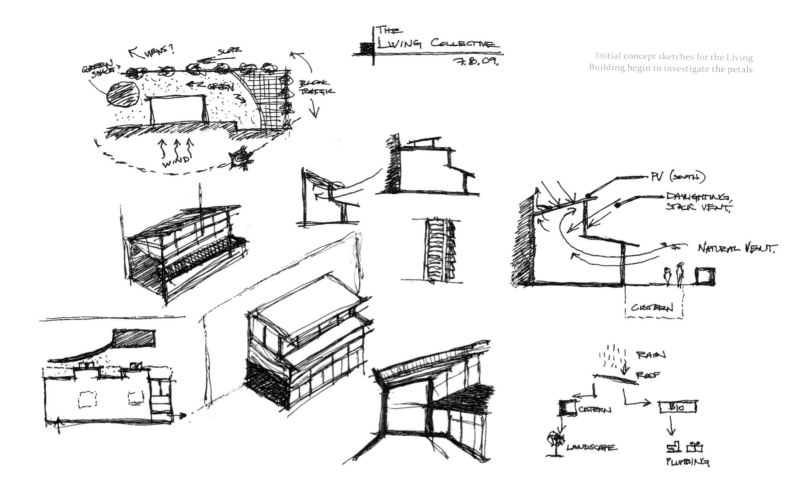

Initial concept sketches for the Living Building begin to investigate the petals

Without knowing about the Living Building Challenge, the earnest wish list the students generated touched on many of the Petals. They were imaginative, open and reflective of how children view science and want to explore it. They want hands-on experiences, and they want to be immersed in nature when they study it.

While some of their wish list items seemed unachievable at first glance, the design team wanted to include each of them and provide a functional aspect to each item. Take the indoor stream wish, for example. In the building industry, professionals work hard to keep water out of buildings, but the Bertschi students had other ideas. They wanted to see a stream flowing by their desks and they did not get consumed with waterproofing details, design standards or precedents. They asked for what they wanted and this opened the minds of the design team to build the solutions that could fulfill those wish lists. Even at this early stage in the project, it was very clear to the team that, "their unbridled thinking and ideas would lead to the most inspiring and educational components of the building," says Stacy. "The process gave the children ownership and creative presence in the building that greatly enhanced its function and its story."

"The students feel a true sense of ownership because so many of their ideas have been incorporated into the Living Building."

JULIE BLYSTAD
Science Specialist,
Bertschi School

43

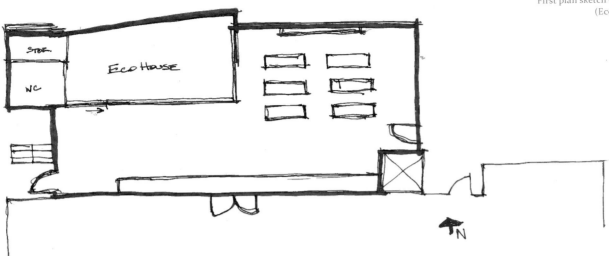

DESIGN PROCESS

**The very first sketches of the design
incorporated the students' ideas.
Some of the first floor plans had the
unmistakable sinusoidal form of a
stream running through the classroom.**

Design options had cisterns inside the building, outside
the building, on the roof and underground. The design
team tried stacks for ventilation and different window
configurations for daylight. There was one green roof
and sometimes there were more. Roof lines were always
slopped to collect rainwater whether in a single shed or
a butterfly form. But no matter how many sketches were
drawn, they always represented the ideas of the students.

The two factors that contributed most greatly to the design
were the constraints of the tight urban site and the existing
church building. Since the Living Building was located on the
north side of the church building, it would be largely shaded
throughout the year. This location presented some obstacles
in both daylighting and photovoltaic (PV) placement. Both of
these factors contributed significantly to the overall design.

Confined by restraints such as building setbacks and other
zoning ordinances, the Ecohouse, one of the most predominant
design features of the building, evolved in stages. The school
had requested a separate greenhouse structure, which the
team named the Ecohouse, to serve their many plant studies,
but zoning codes would not allow this structure type to exist
beyond the property's setback lines. To solve this issue, the Living
Building's final design merged the original Ecohouse concept
with classroom space to create a grand design, transforming
the once typical lean-to backyard structure into a double-
height space that has become the focus of the building's overall
mass. The shape of the Ecohouse intersects with the rectilinear
classroom to link the regularity of academic study and the fluid
investigation and exploration of nature through experimentation.

As the team began to investigate the permitting process for the
project with the City of Seattle's Department of Planning and
Development (DPD), it found that lot coverage development
standards did not apply to this particular zoning designation.
Only development standards listed for institutions (a school
building fits this designation) must be adhered to, which meant
that a Master Use Permit (MUP) was not required for this project.
This exemption made the design process a bit easier in terms
of public participation. Unlike other projects in Seattle that

44

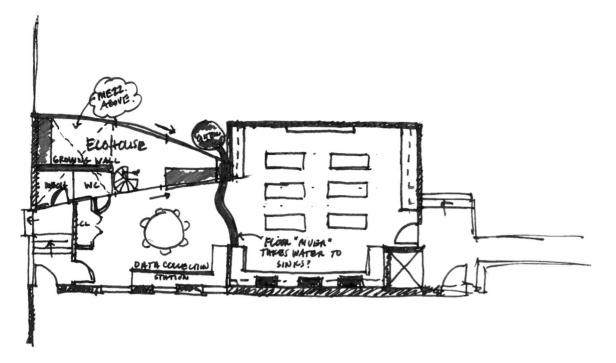

LEFT:
The Living Building plan
begins to take shape

BELOW:
Potable water harvesting
system concept

must follow a MUP process, the project team was not required to hold regular public meetings to present its design and then make changes based on comments from citizens and a city-based design review board. Because the project was following the Living Building Challenge, another benefit was that it was able to follow Seattle DPD's Priority Green permitting process. Taking a huge step to lead the country in sustainable building, Seattle created the Living Building Pilot Program to help the development of twelve Challenge pilot projects in the city. This streamlined permitting process provides projects with reduced permit timelines, better interdepartmental coordination and an integrated plan review. While the Bertschi project did not qualify for Seattle's LBC Pilot because it was not eligible for a MUP, it was able to use the standard Priority Green process that has the same benefits listed above. And, as the first Challenge project for the city, the team was able to help train DPD staff on reviewing Living Building Challenge drawing sets.

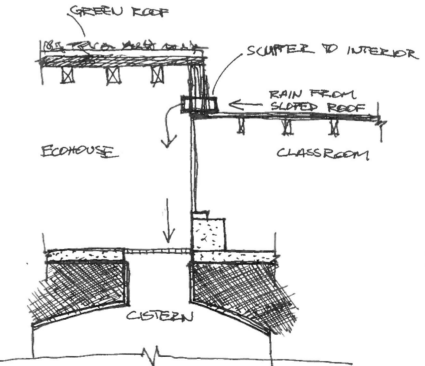

45

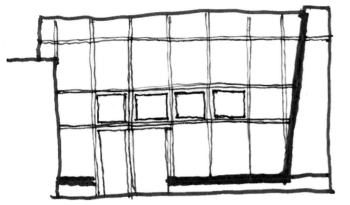

Ecohouse elevation sketch

*"Everybody is here to do the same thing —
a common goal and we're all going to try to
help each other do it in whatever way we can."*

STAN RICHARDSON
Director of Campus Planning, Bertschi School

INTEGRATED
PROJECT DELIVERY

**Integrated project delivery (IPD), also
sometimes referred to as integrated design,
is a project delivery approach that integrates
people, systems, business structures
and practices into a collaborative process.
The idea is that all the disciplines work
together to help create a more seamless
design process and increase overall efficiency.**

Although the project team did not contractually label its
method as integrated project delivery the team followed
this integrated process. From the very first design charrette,
Jason F. McLennan cautioned that the team would not
succeed in creating a Living Building without following an
integrated approach. IPD is necessary for a Living Building
project. The Challenge demands collaboration. It demands
teamwork to create successful sustainable solutions. John
Muir said "when we try to pick out anything by itself, we find
it hitched to everything else in the universe." And that is
exactly what the team discovered with Living Buildings. Each
part is connected to the next, even when they may seem like
opposites. During a project the team might be trying to solve
an urban agriculture issue but finds that its solution depends
on net zero water design, which may affect net zero energy.

Integrated design was a new process for Bertschi School.
Past building projects were very different, operating on
a standard model. But for the Living Building, Stan says,
"It was integrated design both from the aspect of getting
everybody talking about their pieces and how they work
together but also integrated in the common goal of making
it a successful Living Building and making a successful
education facility for young students for science. It fit so well
without us even realizing that's what we were doing."

As the project continued, it became clear that there was
something else that helped to make the process successful.
"Quite frankly, the difference was money. Taking money out
of the picture truly made integrated design a possibility at
such a different level that it couldn't happen any other way,"
Stan reflects. He remembers that, "The biggest driver in the
whole thing was the willingness to learn and people gave way
beyond what they would in any other project." While putting
together a pro bono team was a risk, this spirit was one of
the benefits Stacey and I had hoped would persist through
the project. We were counting on our team of professionals
to use their passions for sustainability and early childhood
education. By having no design fees, we hoped that everyone
would be focused on finding the best sustainable solutions
for a Living Building and the team did not disappoint.

Contractually, the project used the standard American Institute
of Architects (AIA) B101 2007 documents. These documents
were used with few modifications except for noting all design
and reimbursable fees at zero. For consultant agreements,
a KMD-created contract was used. Both of these contracts
provided the same level of legal protection and industry-
wide recognition that typical architectural projects follow.
Construction contractor Skanska was retained separately with
the Bertschi School using the standard AIA G Series documents.

46

The first charrette

THE CHARRETTE AND PROCESS

"I knew that day at the first charrette this was going to be a different process. Everybody was coming at it with an open mind saying, 'I don't know how to do this — we've never done this before and have to figure out how to do it. We have to learn from each other. We have to help each other.' I think that open-minded approach led to integrated design in a way that wouldn't normally happen."

STAN RICHARDSON
Director of Campus Planning,
Bertschi School

As an experienced design team with sustainable projects and LEED work, all members knew the importance of a charrette. A charrette is an initial project team workshop where all stakeholders come together to brainstorm the grand ideas for a particular project. For the Living Building project, team members knew it needed to be something different from what they were all accustomed to. In late September 2009, more than thirty people gathered at Skanska's Seattle office to embark on this Living Building Challenge journey. The participants included the entire design team; Brigitte Bertschi, Head of Bertschi School; Stan Richardson, Director of Campus Planning; Julie Blystadt, Bertschi science teacher, school facilities personnel; the city; the county; and select subcontractors. Even Jason F. McLennan was there.

The challenges of a Living Building demanded a non-traditional approach, including beginning collaboration early. Having subcontractors at the charrette was one of the most beneficial early decisions. It helped the team to get immediate feedback to proposed solutions based on what was currently available in the marketplace.

THE TEAM BEGAN WITH AN AMBITIOUS SET OF GOALS FOR THE PROJECT:

- Celebrate and inspire!

- Create a magical and joyous place

- Create an experience!

- Seek social equity and connections

- Seek true sustainability – go beyond the Imperatives

- Create the next generation's environmentally-aware leaders

- Make a teachable and educational structure – express the building and systems

- Take steps through this project to bring codes in line with technical capacity

- Learn from the fifth graders

- Meet student objectives/give them a voice in the process

- Integrate the campus

- Allow for lessons from the class and building into the rest of students' lives

- Create a developing nation to developed nation connection – use simple technologies from developing nations

- Design a water system that is net zero energy

- Create a nutrient cycle on-site and incorporate urban agriculture

- Add to the community and remember we are not alone!

"The energy in that room was amazing, nobody was bored and it instilled a lot of energy in the project from the very beginning."

STAN RICHARDSON
Director of Campus Planning, Bertschi School

The team began the charrette by presenting each of the Petals of the Living Building Challenge and describing what it would be pursuing in the design of the building. Following a thorough discussion of the Challenge, the charrette team embarked on a creativity exercise, using the Challenge Petals as a framework for ideas about what a Living Building could be and how a particular Petal could be achieved.

Following their inspiration, team members discussed the wish list ideas generated by Bertschi fifth graders and everyone was encouraged to think from a child's perspective "in a real and serious way."

The excitement and enthusiasm among the team members was extraordinary and a range of ideas for every Petal was generated. The building would be a playground for science and a place for textbooks to come alive and team members were striving to make the architecture reflect that vision.

With ideas for every Petal written all over the walls, the list was narrowed, using green, yellow and red dots to represent the level of concern for a particular strategy. From this system a matrix was created to evaluate the next design steps. In subsequent design meetings, the ideas were to develop a complete design to help meet the Challenge Imperatives.

"To have the general contractor and at least two of their subs at the table was pretty impressive."

STAN RICHARDSON
Director of Campus Planning, Bertschi School

The list of donors who made the Living Building a reality hangs in the garden

"*This was a community-wide effort that was embraced and funded in support of innovation.*"

TIFFANY CAREY
Director of Advancement,
Bertschi School

BUILT BY THE PEOPLE

Bertschi School had always planned to build a new science wing; it was part of the 2003 campus master plan. However, there were no plans to build it in the near future when the Restorative Design Collective approached them. And while the Board members had heard about Living Buildings and considered the Challenge for their expansion project, they had not yet decided to take it on. The Restorative Design Collective proposal condensed the school's decision timeline. At that time, the school did not have funding set aside for the project, especially after recently opening the Bertschi Center. As a private school, Bertschi fundraises annually to balance the operating budget and had recently closed the Make Room for Bertschi campaign funding construction of the Bertschi Center. Fortunately, the lack of funding for the science wing did not deter the school's Board. Board members knew their community would support the Living Building Challenge and the lasting educational opportunities it would bring for generations of Bertschi students.

Tiffany Carey, Director of Advancement at Bertschi, was given the critical and considerable task of fundraising for the project. As a Bertschi alumna herself and having worked at the school through high school and college, Tiffany has an in-depth understanding of Bertschi School's mission and connection with its community. She studied science under Julie Blystad for six years at Bertschi, recalling that she's someone who will "ignite curiosity and interest in any child." Tiffany still has a childhood photo hanging in her office of Julie and her building rockets together in 1988.

Soon after the Bertschi School Board approval, Tiffany and the staff launched a $1 million campaign to fund construction of the Living Building. Bertschi Board Member Mary Pembroke Perlin recalls one of her most inspiring moments when the community showed its support for the Living Building. Completely unsolicited, a family foundation sent an anonymous gift of $100,000. The accompanying letter said that the Living Building philosophy was perfectly in keeping with their family's values and their philanthropic goals. Although this was the first major gift in support of the building, it certainly was not the last.

Within this overall campaign, the school opened a mini-campaign, known as Give to Grow, to help raise the final $50,000. This campaign provided the opportunity for anyone in the community to become involved with a gift of $250. At the time the campaign was underway, the weakening economy

49

had become a concern and this smaller campaign allowed more people to contribute. With a gift, the donor's name was engraved on a stepping-stone in the garden. Give to Grow was very successful, raising just over the campaign goal.

Tiffany says that one of the challenges for this campaign was "explaining what a Living Building is and how it differs from LEED. We teach our children to 'dare to be wrong' and to learn from mistakes - this project challenged us to walk our talk." The school worked hard not only to convey the unique aspects of a Living Building to students, but also to the greater adult community. Even with the challenges of the economy and possible donor fatigue coming off the recently completed Bertschi Center, this project mattered to people. It inspired them to give because, as Tiffany says, "it extends learning and is a tangible example of our mission in action. Our curriculum truly drove the project, when oftentimes it's the other way around."

One of the many benefits afforded during this fundraising phase was the opportunity to connect directly with the Bertschi community through a series of events organized by the school and held at the homes of donors. In these intimate settings, Stacy and I were able to have in-depth conversations about what a Living Building would mean for Bertschi. Tiffany says these parties, "offered us the opportunity to convey our dreams for a new science classroom that would push our commitment to sustainable construction further and, more importantly, allow our students to learn in a space that embodies our own curriculum." It was a great honor to be able to work directly with a larger client group; something architects are not often able to do with many large-scale projects.

Similarly, during construction team members were able to spend time in classrooms and talk directly with the students, showing them floor plans and talking about what a Living Building would mean to their science curriculum. "I love that Bertschi allows time to take advantage of exceptional learning opportunities, to step away from the core curriculum to extend learning," says Tiffany. After only a few visits members of the design team would often catch students looking over the plans with their classmates. Without any prompting, design team members could hear students pointing out features on the plans. "Over here is where the composting toilet will be." "This is the ethnobotanical garden that we can help plant," they would say excitedly. Before the building was even under construction, students were gaining an understanding of the project's ambitions and began to learn to read architectural plans at a simple level. But these visits to the school were not only making a difference for Bertschi students, they were having a significant impact on team members as well. The time with the children inspired everyone more after each visit. The school assemblies provided greater insight into the students' hopes for their building and a greater understanding of the school's educational processes. Extra time at the school just made the project that much more enjoyable to be a part of.

Garden stepping-stones from the "Give to Grow" campaign

50

Bertschi students
explore their Ecohouse

LBC PETALS
ARE ACTUALLY
ABOUT PEOPLE

With its simplicity in structure and ideals,
the Living Building Challenge, while not
easy to achieve, is designed to be easily
understood. Following the metaphor of
a flower, the sustainability concepts are
easily mapped through this recognizable
image. This recognition is what makes it
perfect for children. From the students at
Bertschi to adults around the world, the
flower is the great equalizer. Everyone can
think of a floral image and everyone can
find some beauty in a particular species.

As the team certainly found, the Challenge is
about relationships. It is about the relationships
between people and their planet, between people
and their buildings, between the people who
use the building and between those who help
to make them a reality. The Living Building
Challenge helps us all to explore what it means
to be a part of this earth. As each Imperative
is discussed, think about how they relate to
each other and consider the way a flower would
naturally behave. Czechoslovakian poet and
politician Vaclav Havel reminds us that, "We
must draw our standards from the natural world."

PART III

Living Building Challenge at Bertschi

Pursuing the Petals

Bertschi Living Building

Part III: **LIVING BUILDING CHALLENGE AT BERTSCHI**

LEFT: Bertschi students tour their Ecohouse for the first time on opening day.

RIGHT, TOP & BOTTOM: The Living Building is perfect for science experiments.

54

LIVING BUILDING EDUCATION

The following chapters of this book focus on the seven individual
Petals of the Living Building Challenge™ version 2.0:

SITE

Limits to Growth

Urban Agriculture

Habitat Exchange

Car Free Living

WATER

Net Zero Water

Ecological Water Flow

ENERGY

Net Zero Energy

HEALTH

Civilized Environment

Healthy Air

Biophilia

MATERIALS

Red List

Embodied Carbon Footprint

Responsible Industry

Appropriate Sourcing

Conservation + Reuse

EQUITY

Human Scale + Humane Places

Democracy + Social Justice

Rights to Nature

BEAUTY

Beauty + Spirit

Inspiration + Education

THE
SITE
PETAL

Restoring an Urban Site

DO NOT DRINK
NON-POTABLE
WATER

SUMMARY OF THE LIVING BUILDING CHALLENGE VERSION 2.0 SITE PETAL

Petal Intent

The intent of this Petal is to clearly articulate where it is acceptable for people to build, how to protect and restore a place once it has been developed, and to encourage the creation of communities that are once again based on the pedestrian rather than the automobile. Such communities should, in turn, be supported by local and regional agriculture, since no truly "sustainable" community can exist that relies on globally-sourced food production.

Petal Imperatives

- Limits To Growth
- Urban Agriculture
- Habitat Exchange
- Car Free Living

58

The LEED Gold Bertschi Center

AN URBAN SCHOOL

Located in a dense urban neighborhood bordering downtown Seattle, the Bertschi School campus presents a range of challenges for a Living Building project. But for the Site Petal, it also presents a great deal of opportunities. Our team quickly learned that every square foot of the site would be important to creating a functioning Living Building since so many of the Imperatives are directly or indirectly tied to the site.

In 2009, Bertschi School had nearly completed its campus master plan. Like many other urban schools across the country, open space was at a premium. The school had chosen, as with the majority of their expansion projects, to renovate rather than to demolish. But even with this restorative approach there was very little open space remaining except for the far north end of the block-long campus.

The site where the Living Building now stands was once an asphalt-covered play court. Not only did this present a site that supported stormwater runoff and introduced an unnatural surface, it did not promote nature. There was no natural water infiltration, no plant life growing and no urban sanctuary. And while the site had been previously developed for generations, it needed an improvement; a restorative improvement.

KENT VALLEY, WASHINGTON
1965

KENT VALLEY, WASHINGTON
1996

IMPERATIVE:
LIMITS TO GROWTH

Limits to Growth is one of the few Imperatives that resembles a LEED Credit. Here, projects are required to be built on a previously developed site and Bertschi School was the perfect example of an urban site that was ready for restoration. Just like any developed area on earth, Puget Sound has its own examples of continually expanding built environments at the expense of nature.

This development can be traced to the ever expanding population in Washington State. If current trends continue, by 2045 we may have 11 million people in our state, nearly double the population we have today.[16] An increase in population, especially this dramatic, has wide-ranging impacts from natural resources to economics. About half the land area of Washington State is covered in forests and in the last fifty years, we have lost more than two-thirds of these old-growth forests to development.[17] Of course, there are a variety of reasons for a population swell and, in turn, the deforestation of land for the built environment. A large part of this deforestation is due to economics and how we value nature. For example, in Washington State, if you exclude the value of timber, it is not uncommon for the value

of land zoned as residential to be worth more than tenfold the value of comparably sized timber land. This devaluing of our natural resources has resulted in the loss of more than 2.3 million acres of forest lands that have been converted to other uses or designations in the last thirty years. If we just look at the loss of timber lands from 1979 to 1989 that were converted from prime forest zone, we see startling statistics. Urban expansion was responsible for about 48 percent of this forest conversion, rights-of-way accounted for about 28 percent and agricultural uses made up the other approximately 24 percent.[18]

It is clear that even in what is considered to be a mostly environmentally conscious state and one with abundant natural resources, the growth of urban development is a threat to so many of our valuable ecosystems. Limits to growth are necessary.

16 Blanche Sobottke, ed. *Our Changing Nature: Natural Resource Trends in Washington State.* Rep. N.p.: n.p., n.d. 1998.
17 Ibid.
18 Ibid.

60

URBAN AGRICULTURE

One of the most distinctive Imperatives of the Living Building Challenge requires new building projects to provide urban agriculture. Based on a project's scale and density, known as the FAR or Floor Area Ratio, each project has a different requirement. FAR is the ratio between the site area and a building's floor area. The requirements are unique to each city's zoning code and help determine the massing of a building and a particular amount of air space and daylight penetration around a design.

For Bertschi, this meant that nearly 37 percent of the site, more than 1,200 square feet, was to be dedicated to urban agriculture. This proviso presented a challenge on a north-facing, small urban site but we had a great team in place to achieve it.

While the project was originally registered with the International Living Future Institute (ILFI) under the most current version of the Challenge at the time, version 1.3, this version had no urban agriculture requirement. However, we had already decided to include a small amount of food production to serve

Ethnobotanical plant identification by QR Code

SNOW BERRY

61

The Site Petal: RESTORING AN URBAN SITE

> *"My design work has always been driven by big ideas in ecological restoration. I am solution oriented. Having worked in urban agriculture for many years, I felt I could help design a space for the school that built on my experiences in more traditional urban agriculture models and yet develop something that would inspire the next generations of naturalists, urban farmers and botanists to think outside of the box."*

BROOKE SULLIVAN
Restoration Ecologist and Arborist, Back to Nature Design

as a demonstration piece. Since the project began, the team had the expertise of landscape architects from GGLO. But talking with others in the sustainable community, we began to realize the need for an arborist and an agriculture specialist. At that time, urban agriculture was one of the great emerging topics in architectural sustainability. This topic was particularly germane to Seattle where we have a range of experts in the field. In October 2009, we reached out to Brooke Sullivan who is a restoration ecologist, landscape designer and certified arborist. Like all the other team members before her, she agreed to join our group immediately to begin visioning and concept development.

In early November, soon after the first meeting with Brooke, the team received the exciting news that it had been waiting for. The newest version of the Challenge had been released and included a new Imperative for Urban Agriculture. Immediately, the team began to analyze the Imperative language and came up with a list of questions that we needed to clarify with ILFI. To begin with, we needed a simple definition of what urban agriculture meant to them. As an expert, Brooke was immediately able to consider the history of agriculture and its development 10,000 years ago. While that sounds like it may be out of the scope of the Imperative's

intent, the team felt it was necessary to determine the many different aspects of agriculture that could apply, ranging from sustainable husbandry to aquaculture. One of the other important questions for our team was how urban agriculture would be measured. In an urban site, this was particularly important as we had hoped to use vertical space to supplement horizontal plantings. In small urban sites, meaningful agriculture can be difficult to achieve. Brooke says that, "traditional models of urban agriculture, which have developed from larger farm-based methods, have basically become miniaturized for the smaller lots and community gardens found in cities — and there are already a lot of them. The organic gardening movement has also been influential more recently in residential and community-based agriculture. Urban food gardens in the past have largely been created for reasons of food security (often in poorer communities and in war times), and more recently for community/educational enrichment."

As the team continued to work out design options, Brooke and the GGLO team of Mark and Zack came up with a unique design response to create an ethnobotanical garden. The term ethnobotanical comes from ethnobotany: the study of how people

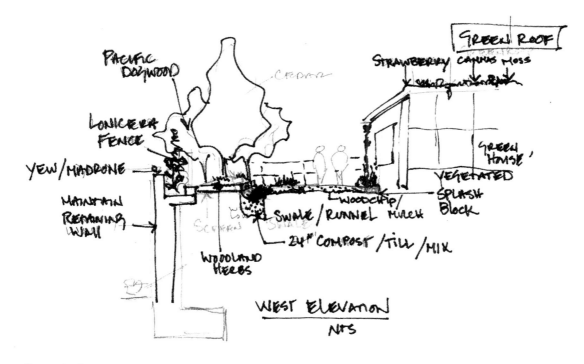

Within the sketch:
PACIFIC DOGWOOD
CEDAR
LONICERA FENCE
YEW/MADRONE
MAINTAIN RETAINING WALL
WOODLAND HERBS
SWALE/RUNNEL
24" COMPOST/TILL/MIX
WOODCHIP/MULCH
GREEN ROOF
STRAWBERRY CANVUS MOSS
GREEN HOUSE
VEGETATED
SPLASH BLOCK
WEST ELEVATION
NTS

of a particular culture and region (in Bertschi School's case, Coastal Salish Tribes) make use of indigenous (native) plants.[19] Essentially, it is the relationship between people and plants.

The team felt that a broader use of urban agriculture that added a physical component of Northwest native cultures was a perfect fit for the school. It turns out that most of the plants used by Northwest natives for food, fiber and medicine are shade-tolerant, which worked well for the project's north shaded site. "Ultimately, I felt a garden that explored the cultivation of native plants for food and honored the traditions of indigenous Salish peoples would be the most stimulating use of the garden space for these children," recalled Brooke. "I saw it as an opportunity for the children to further educate their parents and other friends about native plants and native peoples."

Native plants are key components of pre-European "productive landscapes" and provide lessons both in the variety of productive landscapes and the ingenuity of Native peoples. Since the idea of pursuing ethnobotany along with urban agriculture was a new strategy, the team needed to get acceptance from ILFI to ensure it

met the Imperative's requirements. In her appeal to ILFI, Brooke wrote: "Historically, native plants and animals in our region provided plentiful foods all year for the early human inhabitants of our land, and yet their edible and medicinal uses are little known and practiced today. Foods were gathered seasonally, beginning in early spring and continuing into the late fall. Native plants provided materials for clothing, ceremony, baskets, canoes, homes and technology. Native plants also provided a variety of fresh bark, roots, leaves, nuts and fruit that were collected for food and medicines. Many plants were also known to have spiritual meaning and energy."

In accordance with the official procedure, the team offered its proposal to ILFI's online Dialogue and it was accepted as a new implementation path for this Imperative including the option of counting vertical areas of agriculture. The online Dialogue is a discussion forum for specific questions about Imperatives, which allows teams to consult with ILFI staff. This acceptance was a great success for our team.

19 www.fs.fed.us/wildflowers/ethnobotany/index.shtml

63

PLANTING PLAN

LIMIT OF WORK

SOIL PREPARATION AND GRADING ONLY - PLANTING LAYOUT SHOWN FOR REFERENCE ONLY

MOSS MAT TYPE 2

MOSS MAT TYPE 3

METAL EDGE SEPARATING MAT TYPES, TYP - LAYOUT TO BE COORDINATED IN FIELD WITH LANDSCAPE ARCH

ONLY GREEN ROOF PLANTING INCLUDED IN CONTRACT - REMAINING PLANTING LAYOUT AND SCHEDULE SHOWN FOR REFERENCE ONLY

MOSS MAT TYPE 1

LIMIT OF WORK

PLANTING LIMIT OF WORK

LIMIT OF WORK

TREES	BOTANICAL NAME	COMMON NAME	VINE/ESPALIER	BOTANICAL NAME	COMMON NAME

TREES

BOTANICAL NAME	COMMON NAME
Cornus nuttallii Native	Western Flowering Dogwood

SHRUBS

	BOTANICAL NAME	COMMON NAME
	Cornus serica 'Kelseyi' DWARF CULTIVAR OF NATIVE	Kelseyi Dogwood
	Ledum glandulosum LEAVES USED FOR TEA	Western Labrador Tea
	Oemleria cerasiformis NATIVE WITH EDIBLE FRUIT	Indian Plum
	Polystichum munitum NATIVE	Western Sword Fern
	Symphoricarpos albus NATIVE	Common White Snowberry
	Vaccinium ovatum 'Thunderbird' NATIVE WITH EDIBLE FRUIT	Evergreen Huckleberry

VINE/ESPALIER

	BOTANICAL NAME	COMMON NAME
⊘2	Actinidia argula 'Issai' EDIBLE FRUIT	Hardy Kiwi
⊘2	Vitis vinifera EDIBLE FRUIT	Grape

GROUND COVERS

	BOTANICAL NAME	COMMON NAME
⊘2	Asarum caudatum EDIBLE ROOT	British Columbia Wild Ginger
	Blechnum spicant NATIVE	Deer Fern

64

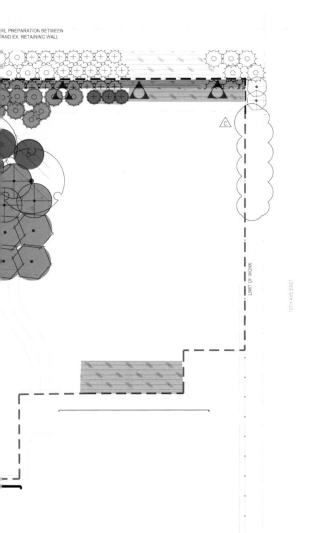

SOIL PREPARATION BETWEEN
AND EX. RETAINING WALL

LIMIT OF WORK

10TH AVE EAST

LBC 2.0 IMPERATIVE: URBAN AGRICULTURE

SUMMARY TABLE	
FLOOR AREA RATIO:	.025 – 0.49
% OF PROJECT AREA REQUIRED FOR AG:	30%
TOTAL SITE AREA:	3,380 SF
AREA REQUIRED FOR AG:	**1,014 SF**
ON-SITE AGRICULTURAL AREAS PROVIDED	
EDIBLE ETHNOBOTANICAL PLANTS	153 SF
NON-EDIBLE ETHNOBOTANICAL PLANTS	93 SF
EDIBLE & NON-EDIBLE ETHNOBOTANICAL PLANTS	230 SF
6FT HT. GREEN WALL W/ FRUITING VINES	606 SF
OFF-SITE AGRICULTURAL AREAS PROVIDED	
VEGETABLE GARDEN (NOT PICTURED)	161 SF
TOTAL AGRICULTURAL AREAS PROVIDED:	**1,243 SF**

Edible Ethnobotanical
Plant Area (153 SF)

Edible & Non-edible
Ethnobotanical Plant
Area (230 SF)

Non-edible Ethnobotanical
Plant Area (93 SF)

6FT HT. Green Wall w/
Fruiting Vines (606 SF)

Green Roof (522 SF)

GROUND COVERS | **BOTANICAL NAME** | **COMMON NAME**

Elymus glaucus
RAIN GARDEN PLANT | Blue Wildrye

Deschampsia cespitosa
RAIN GARDEN PLANT | Tufted Hair Grass

Elymus glaucus
RAIN GARDEN PLANT | Blue Wildrye

Fragaria vesca
EDIBLE FRUIT | Woodland Strawberry

Gaultheria shallon
EDIBLE FRUIT | Salal

Mahonia repens
EDIBLE FRUIT | Creeping Mahonia

Vaccinium vitis-idaea
EDIBLE FRUIT | Lingonberry

GREEN ROOF

Pacific Northwest Sedum Mix #1

Pacific Northwest Sedum Mix #2

Pacific Northwest Sedum Mix #3

65

SCIENTIFIC NAME	COMMON NAME
Ledum groenlandicum 'Oeder'	Bog Labrador Tea
Vaccinium ovatum 'Thunderbird'	Evergreen Huckleberry
Vaccinium x 'Northsky'	Northsky Highbush Blueberry
Gaultheria shallon	Salal
Mahonia repens	Creeping Oregon Grape
Vaccinium vitis-idaea	Lingonberry
Actinidia arguta 'Issai'	Hardy Kiwi Vine
Asarum caudatum	Wild Ginger
Camassia quamash	Common Camas
Fragaria vesca	Woodland Strawberry
Vitis 'Buffalo'	Buffalo Grape
Symphoricarpus albus	Common Snowberry
Oemleria cerasiformis	Indian Plum

TOP:
Bertschi art students paint with tools they fashioned from their garden.

BOTTOM:
Student-created art tools

STUDENT GARDENERS

In February 2011, less than two weeks before the building would open, we gathered the students to plant their own garden. "The ground was practically frozen," Mark recalls. "The sun was beaming and the children were bristling with enthusiasm and pride."

The day began with the youngest Bertschi students, the kindergartners. Both Mark and Zack started the planting exercise with a few simple tips on how to properly plant. Then, small groups of students grabbed their plants of choice, dug the proper hole they were just instructed on and carefully set the native flora into their new home. This process repeated through each grade level throughout the day. Mark, Zack, Stacy, Stan and I got to spend some time with each of these eager students as they took ownership of their new ethnobotanical garden. Of course, while we used this interactive participation for educational reasons, there was also a budgetary benefit for the project. Having the students help plant some of the garden saved on the labor from a landscaping contractor. While this was a rewarding day to be sure, Mark says that, "some of the best moments were seeing the children eagerly bringing their parents back into the garden to point out the plants they had planted, describe what they were, and the sense of accomplishment that brought them." These inspirational and educational themes are what our team would strive for throughout the project.

Perhaps one of the most intriguing aspects of this ethnobotanical garden was the collaboration with Bertschi's art department. Less than a year after planting, the garden began to produce. Vines filled with grapes were climbing the fences, grasses stood tall, ferns and moss filled in and blueberries, snowberries and lingonberries flourished. After harvesting the huckleberries and elderberries, students ground them into uniform liquids of various color paints using a mortar and pestle. With grasses and sticks gathered from the garden, students fashioned paint brushes from a split branch bound with bark strips just as the Natives have done for centuries. With these naturally made art supplies, Bertschi students were creating beautiful, unique pieces of art. Bertschi art teacher Maria Grade guided the students, helping them to, "use crushed leaves to add dark green smudges and experiment with different found materials such as bark pieces and soil. Some students then invented a type of scroll that combined their brush and painting together." It was something that team members talked about as a feature of the garden and were touched when they finally saw it all come to fruition.

The garden holds many more opportunities for the students and Maria to continue to investigate nature. Maria plans, "potential visual arts lessons centered on the ethnobotanical garden including a wide range of culture-based, age-appropriate lessons, integrating concepts and aligning content from many curricula. Examples include basket weaving, wool-dyeing, clay leaf fossil impressions, heliographic printmaking, musical instruments, papermaking, miniature terrariums and brass rubbings. Other explorations include how moss, topiary deviations, decomposition, natural patinas and fading surfaces by sunlight can be used for personal self-expression." But like most of us who have experienced Bertschi's Living Building, the most powerful moments are seen through the eyes of the students. For Maria, these moments came through observing very simple interactions. Some of her favorite moments were: "seeing and hearing students become discerning caretakers and harvesters of natural materials — as reflected in their on-site conversations with each other. They were finding their own method to hold the handmade brushes. They learned to apply the right amount of pressure and ink to create a long line on the paper and then shared their technique with other students. Seeing how they noticed the color of the berries' ink being distinct to each species and how it related to ripeness and optimal harvest time." This is what the ethnobotanical garden was designed to do.

The unique ethnobotanical plants included in the garden were in addition to food producing species. To provide students with a greater understanding of organic farming with a connection to the land and the importance of growing one's own food, they maintain a vegetable garden. Since our Living Building site is located to the north of the three-story church building, traditional urban vegetables would not be successful in the reduced sunlight exposure.

Bertschi's organic garden is a hands-on program designed by GGLO that helps educate students about the values of organic farming, connection to the land and the importance of growing one's own food. A small vegetable garden was constructed as part of the Living Building project but it is located outside the project boundary in a different area of the school's campus. The garden is carefully planned to grow a wide variety of seasonal produce appropriate to Seattle's climate. It shifts and changes from season to season as the classes seed, grow, harvest and rotate crops each year. The harvest from the garden is utilized as snacks in the after school and summer programs. In the fall of 2012, students harvested vegetables and made a delicious potato leek soup and kale salad.

This outdoor classroom enhances student learning across disciplines, helping to integrate science, social studies, geography, math and literature as the garden prompts students to consider their relationship with food and the natural environment. Bertschi students are learning

Every student learned how to plant a part of their garden

68

valuable lessons about urban food production and social justice through humanitarian aid programs.

Local Master Gardeners and urban agriculture experts from Seattle Tilth (a non-profit organic gardening and urban ecology organization with classes, demonstration gardens, children's programs and community events) work with students so they can learn to maintain and nurture the garden. Some of the garden lessons include: learning the cycle of plants from seed to seed, planting in pots (to grow at school and bring home), on-site food waste collection and composting, maintenance of worm bins, learning about commonly found garden insects, garden maintenance including winterizing, learning to identify ripe vegetables and fruits, and harvesting and cooking the products from the garden.

During the first school year when the building was in operation, the art students worked with GGLO to create further educational opportunities for the garden. Born out of a casual conversation, Mark Sindell from GGLO helped the school develop an electronic plant database conceived by Stan Richardson. This database outlines detailed information, including photos of how each plant looks through the seasons. The online guide shows the cycle of each plant from seed to fruit as well as its location, type and appeal to the senses. The exciting and unique feature of the database system is that natural looking rocks with leaf impressions were molded with clay to provide plant identification labels and a quick response or QR code. When students walk through the garden and encounter a plant and its label, they can scan the QR code with their school-provided iPads to immediately access the wealth of information in the digital database. A scan of the code shows the plant's common and scientific names and has a link to the school's website with information about how Native people use these plants. This type of educational link is important as it helps further students' understanding of technology and allows them to stay connected to nature at the same time. Mark believes that this "is one of the most popular and powerful learning tools of the project, and should be a model implemented in all educational and publicly accessible urban gardens in the future."

Bertschi's ethnobotanical garden, like so many other urban plantings, can provide many benefits for both humans and the environment. Like so many of the Imperatives, the Urban

Planting the garden

Agriculture Imperative provided lessons not just for the students, but for the project team as well. Through the process, Mark learned that "there is a great symbiotic relationship between native ecology, native peoples, history, food, education and pride." As our global population increases, food resources and food security will become more pressing issues. It is important to teach future generations ways to avert these problems. We all have so many hopes for the children at Bertschi School and Brooke expressed this very clearly. She hopes the students will, "see the inherent benefits of native plants for all beings, not just for the food they can provide to us in the woods, but also for the protection and food they offer our own native fauna, which in turn become food for other animals, including humans." We are all part of the natural world and sometimes these connections are easiest to see when we connect with our gardens.

69

All photos: Naches Forest Restoration in Washington's Cascade Mountains

IMPERATIVE:
HABITAT EXCHANGE

While the most sustainable choice we can make for the environment is not to build at all, it is unrealistic to expect that no additional buildings will ever be developed. The Habitat Exchange Imperative helps account for this reality by offsetting an equal area of land for conservation to match the amount that was developed for the project. While this may seem like a straightforward Imperative, it proved to be much more complicated — and rewarding — than we had anticipated.

In November 2010, the project team began reaching out to the Cascade Land Trust. One of the first issues the team ran into was that these agencies were not yet familiar with the Habitat Exchange requirements of the Living Building Challenge. The team worked with ILFI to help further clarify some of the detailed requirements. The idea of the land purchase is to support an area that has not yet been protected, so simply donating to an organization that purchased land is not enough. With this information, the team turned to the experts at the Nature Conservancy (which has a great Northwest presence) and met Melissa Laird, the Associate Director of Philanthropy.

Bertschi School was attracted to The Nature Conservancy because it had a few large protection areas that were a relatively short drive from the school. We first began with one of the Conservancy's recent land acquisitions of 4,000 acres at Point Susan Bay near Whidbey Island in Puget Sound. Some of the focus of this protection area was bird and fish sanctuary as well as elimination of invasive plant species. Unfortunately, the team determined that the land purchase by the Conservancy was not recent enough to qualify for the Imperative.

Over several months we worked with The Nature Conservancy, identifying other possible options but continually ran into specific Imperative requirements we could not meet. Finally,

70

after a year of research, we found a diverse alpine landscape as part of the Naches Forest Restoration in Washington's Cascade Mountains. The Nature Conservancy had just completed a project to purchase 10,000 acres for protection and restoration which will be transferred to the Washington Department of Fish and Wildlife. Nestled within the Cascade Mountains, this mountainous terrain is home to a variety of wildlife including mountain goats, sheep, elk and black bear. Several streams supporting native fish such as cutthroat, rainbow and bull trout flourish here. This varied landscape of basalt cliffs, canyons, forests and shrub-steppe experiences all four seasons in Washington with endless fields of wildflowers in the summer to dense snow-covered peaks in the winter.

While the Habitat Exchange requires that only the amount of land equal in area to what was developed for the project be protected, Bertschi School chose to protect three times that amount. The land is close enough to the school that staff will be able to take students on field trips to visit the land the school protects. For Bertschi, the Habitat Exchange has become another way for students to be immersed in the nature they are learning about and helping to protect.

IMPERATIVE:
CAR FREE LIVING

This Imperative is focused on contributing to the development of walkable, pedestrian-oriented communities. For an elementary school campus that was not adding students, teachers or staff with the new science wing, this was perhaps the easiest Imperative to achieve.

No new parking was provided with this project. Although it was rather simple for our team to achieve this Imperative, other Living Building Challenge projects, particularly those in urban areas, can find great resistance in this regard. Many communities are reluctant to add people in new buildings without providing a calculated amount of parking to handle the increased population. Without valid public transportation options or properly designed urban environments to support healthy working and living communities, car free living might be a difficult Imperative to overcome for some other projects.

71

THE WATER PETAL

The Hydrologic Cycle Comes to Life

Bertschi students investigate
collected rainwater flowing
through their classroom

73

The Water Petal: THE HYDROLOGIC CYCLE COMES TO LIFE

SUMMARY OF THE LIVING BUILDING CHALLENGE VERSION 2.0 WATER PETAL

Petal Intent

The intent of the Water Petal is to realign how people use water and redefine "waste" in the built environment, so that water is respected as a precious resource. Scarcity of potable water is quickly becoming a serious issue as many countries around the world face severe shortages and compromised water quality. Even regions that have avoided the majority of these problems to date due to a historical presence of abundant fresh water are at risk: the impacts of climate change, highly unsustainable water use patterns, and the continued drawdown of major aquifers portent significant problems ahead.

Petal Imperatives

• Net Zero Water
• Ecological Water Flow

Classroom and runnel

A RIVER IN THE CLASSROOM

The Water Petal is one of my favorite parts of the Living Building Challenge. It is also one of the most difficult but has the opportunity to be one of the most rewarding Petals. Through the exploration and implementation of design features aimed to achieve net zero water, the interaction between water and people can be magical.

Water has long been a part of our culture, our history and our recreation. Even throughout the Bible, many sacred stories have water as a central theme. Studies that merely focused on images of natural and built environments with water showed that people preferred and associated with more positive affect than those without water.[20] Other research has concluded that there are numerous human health benefits when people simply view natural water bodies. These include positive benefits on emotional states,[21] lower fear and anger, greater stress reduction and heart rate deceleration.[22]

Puget Sound and Cascadia are the perfect natural inspiration for the Water Petal as this area is blessed with an abundance of water in so many beautiful forms. This abundance leads to a mismanagement of water resources, however. While we may receive steady recharge of our water resources in the winter from rain and snowfall, the summer seasons usually experience long periods of dryness. These natural patterns are only a problem if humans use this water in a wasteful manner.[23] From Elliott Bay, which meets the skyscrapers of downtown Seattle, to the rainforest less than 100 miles away, water defines the northwest. Although the average annual precipitation in the Puget Sound region is an estimated

20 White, Mathew, Amanda Smith, Kelly Humphryes, Sabine Pahl, Deborah Snelling, and Michael Depledge. "Blue Space: The Importance of Water for Preference, Affect, and Restorativeness Ratings of Natural and Built Scenes." *Journal of Environmental Psychology* 30.4 (2010): 482-93. Print.
21 Ulrich, R.S., 1981. Natural versus urban scenes. Some psychological effects. Environment and Behavior 13, 523–556.
22 Ulrich, R.S., 1981. Natural versus urban scenes. Some psychological effects. Environment and Behavior 13,523–556.

23 Blanche Sobottke, ed. Our Changing Nature: *Natural Resource Trends in Washington State*. Rep. N.p.: n.p., n.d. 1998.

Potable water cistern installation under the Ecohouse

2.5 trillion gallons and freshwater streams flow into the Sound at a rate of 1.5 trillion gallons per year, "one-quarter of the state's watersheds do not have enough water to meet the needs of both people and fish."[24] Conserving and reusing water, even in the Pacific Northwest, is imperative.

The design responses for the Water Petal at Bertschi were truly inspired by the students. Here, the students asked for a river in the classroom with removable glass tiles. With one of their very first requests for what a building about nature could be, the students wanted to bring the powerful river element directly inside. Just the way the Bertschi students are affected by water, I remember from my childhood being fascinated with rivers. I recall building little ones in the sandbox or at the beach and watching water flow over the soil or sand I piled up. From a very early age water can evoke so many strong emotions that can last for years. For me, it was one of the primary reasons I felt called away from Texas to live in the Puget Sound region and see water each day.

The students' wish for the stream was very influential to our team. From the outset, the team wanted to keep the stream in

the project but we had to come up with a functional reason for its inclusion. It quickly became clear that we could incorporate the stream into a runnel to transport captured rainwater.

I recalled having seen an interior runnel in the floor of a retail store in downtown Seattle. This pebble-lined, glass-covered runnel wound its way through the entire store carrying water to a decorative fountain. This installation became our inspiration. Coincidentally, this store was in the process of closing and the interior was to be demolished. Through various connections, we worked with the building's owner to arrange site visits to investigate the runnel's construction as well as the possibility of salvaging it. After all, we were building a sustainable building and one of the best ways to procure materials is through reuse. Our team spent many hours trying to determine the condition of the materials in that runnel and if any of them could be reused on our project. Visiting the store proved to be helpful because one of the main issues we noted on this design was the tendency for the glass panels to become covered in condensation. This flaw was something our design for Bertschi would need to avoid. With the condition of the store's runnel and the effort that would need to be expended to adapt the materials to our design, the team determined the only salvageable items were the numerous pebbles lining the runnel and the large decorative fountain.

The process for designing the runnel was quite lengthy. As architects, we spend a lot of time crafting building details to keep water out of buildings. But for the runnel, we not only wanted to have water in the space, but also to bring it from outside and allow it to flow through the classroom floor slab. Since there are not many precedents for this type of feature, we had to work to determine the appropriate dimensions for the runnel. It had to be deep enough so a heavy rainfall would

24 MacGregor, Barbara, and Blanche Sobottke, eds. *Changing Our Water Ways: Trends in Washington's Water System.* Rep. N.p.: n.p., n.d. Dec. 2000.

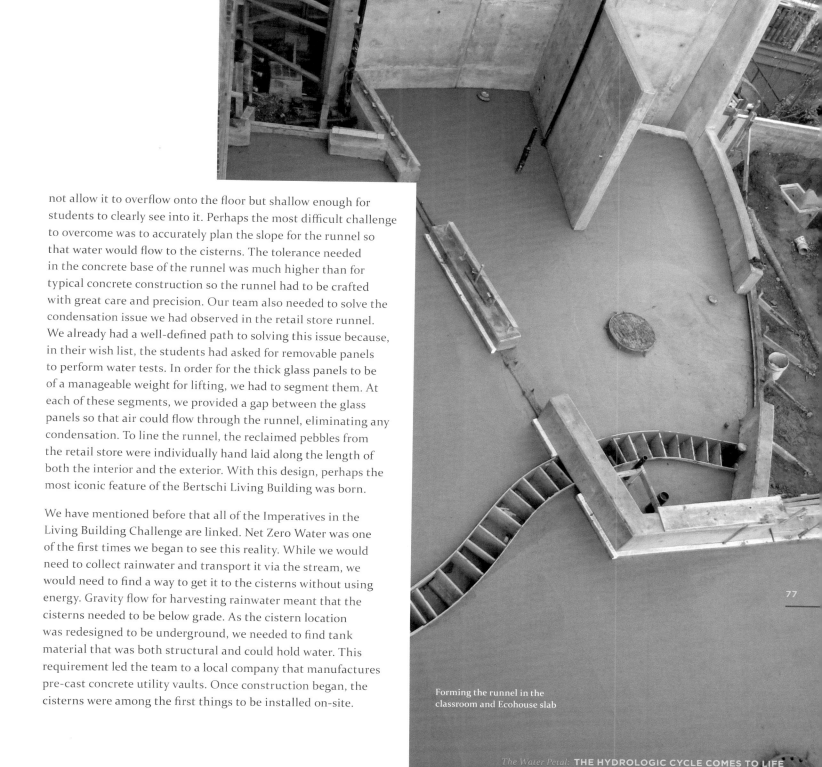

not allow it to overflow onto the floor but shallow enough for students to clearly see into it. Perhaps the most difficult challenge to overcome was to accurately plan the slope for the runnel so that water would flow to the cisterns. The tolerance needed in the concrete base of the runnel was much higher than for typical concrete construction so the runnel had to be crafted with great care and precision. Our team also needed to solve the condensation issue we had observed in the retail store runnel. We already had a well-defined path to solving this issue because, in their wish list, the students had asked for removable panels to perform water tests. In order for the thick glass panels to be of a manageable weight for lifting, we had to segment them. At each of these segments, we provided a gap between the glass panels so that air could flow through the runnel, eliminating any condensation. To line the runnel, the reclaimed pebbles from the retail store were individually hand laid along the length of both the interior and the exterior. With this design, perhaps the most iconic feature of the Bertschi Living Building was born.

We have mentioned before that all of the Imperatives in the Living Building Challenge are linked. Net Zero Water was one of the first times we began to see this reality. While we would need to collect rainwater and transport it via the stream, we would need to find a way to get it to the cisterns without using energy. Gravity flow for harvesting rainwater meant that the cisterns needed to be below grade. As the cistern location was redesigned to be underground, we needed to find tank material that was both structural and could hold water. This requirement led the team to a local company that manufactures pre-cast concrete utility vaults. Once construction began, the cisterns were among the first things to be installed on-site.

Forming the runnel in the classroom and Ecohouse slab

1. Rainwater is collected from roofs and funneled through downspouts and rain leaders into the runnel in the floor of the building.

2. Rainwater is collected in the potable water cistern.

3. Cistern fills and overflows into the exterior runnel.

4. Water is collected in the irrigation cistern outside.

5. Cistern fills and backflows into the exterior runnel.

6. Runnel overflows and infiltrates into the rain garden.

When investigations into the Water Petal began for Bertschi, 2020 Engineers performed detailed calculations to determine the amount of water the building would need for both potable and irrigation needs throughout the year. Essentially, both Mark and Colleen from 2020 designed the systems to achieve the Net Zero Water and Ecological Water Flow Imperatives. Unlike the typical scope of civil engineers, most of their work occurred within the envelope of the Bertschi building. This was one of the many examples of our integrated design process which Colleen describes as, "necessary and natural." Her idea to achieve the Water Petal was to "illustrate how water is used within a building while operating within the carrying capacity of the site. I really saw Bertschi as an opportunity to reconnect with how we meet our basic needs through interactive experience," says Colleen.

2020 Engineering performed hydrologic calculations using the Western Washington Hydrology Model, version 3. This software contains over fifty years of historic rainfall data, and has been calibrated to calculate site-specific rainfall, evaporation and infiltration parameters. They extrapolated data from these models into project-specific spreadsheets to help determine our design parameters. Along with this model,

2020 researched the average water usage of similarly sized schools, interviewed Bertschi teachers and maintenance staff about their water use habits and needs and adjusted demand estimates to reflect our planned water-conserving fixtures. Once an overall picture of a water use estimate became clear, we also discussed strategies for further water conservation to help reduce overall consumption. With all of this data, a daily demand was calculated and used to determine the necessary volume of storage needed to supply enough water year-round based on rainfall. Our team determined that the average potable water use for the building would be about 2.8 gallons per person per day for a total daily use of about fifty-six gallons per day. For the irrigation demands, 2020 discussed estimated quantities with GGLO, the landscape architect, along with nurseries and botanists and applied estimated indoor evaporation rates based on the type of irrigation system to be installed. This approach helped to determine a weekly irrigation demand that was used to calculate the necessary volume of storage needed to supply enough water for an entire year based on rainfall.

In a true case of form follows function, often a necessity in sustainable design, the main roof of the Bertschi building is a

78

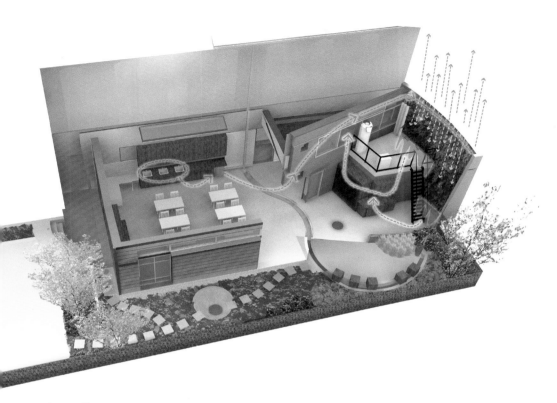

1. Sinks pull water from the potable water cistern.

2. Greywater drains from the sinks into Aqua2 greywater filter box.

3. Greywater is pumped from the filter box to the green wall and delivered by drip irrigation to the plants.

4. Greywater is transpired by the living wall plant material.

5. Any remaining greywater is recycled back through the system until completely eliminated.

butterfly shape to funnel rainwater to rain leaders directly inside the building. Since we also had the benefit of being connected to the existing church building, we also captured rainwater from half of that roof. A variety of filters are included with the system to help remove any particulates or debris that may enter the system from the collected rainwater. The rain leader that brings the church roof water into the science room is the start of the runnel in the floor. The City of Seattle recognizes rainwater cisterns as structures and requires their size to be counted in building square footage calculations. In order to fit our two cisterns on the tight urban site while meeting zoning codes prohibiting the exposed size of cistern we would need on-site, we located them below grade. To save space and materials, the primary potable cistern is located in the floor of the Ecohouse. Here, this 2500 gallon tank is closest to the sinks that will draw its water. And with a location inside the building, students can easily explore the cistern's equipment and perform various water studies. As the potable water cistern fills with water, it will overflow back into the runnel which continues outside into the garden. From here, water flows into the 2700 gallon irrigation cistern and, as that fills, the water backs up into the exterior runnel ultimately overflowing and infiltrating into the rain garden.

This process provides one of the most important educational aspects of Bertschi's water system. It is a representation of the hydrologic cycle right in the classroom. The students are able to see how rainwater is collected from the atmosphere, enters a stream, is used as needed and then discharged back into the water table to begin the cycle all over again. And all of this happens right next to the students' desks. At the grand opening of the building, our team was torn about the weather. We could not decide if we wanted it to rain so the runnel would fill or be sunny for the tour. Now that the building is occupied, the students are just as conflicted each day as they wait for the water to flow through their stream.

Although the Water Petal may be one of the most beautiful parts of the Challenge, it is certainly not without controversy. Once rainwater has been captured for use in the building, it must be treated to potable standards. Currently, the Washington State Department of Health, which is the state agency that oversees drinking water, does not allow commercial buildings to treat rainwater to potable standards for human consumption. In fact, it was only recently, in October 2009, that the Washington Department of Ecology lifted the long-time water rights ban

Students investigate the potable water cistern and take measurements

on rooftop rainwater harvesting. Previously, it had been illegal to collect rainwater even from one's own residential roof.

For a commercial building in Washington State to provide its own water supply for more than fifteen service connections or to more than twenty-five individuals regularly, it is must be classified as a Group A Public Water System. For a new Group A water system to be allowed, permission must be granted from any existing public water system within the same service area. Past experience has shown that water purveyors will not often allow a new Group A water system within their service area. This was one of the first permitting challenges our team encountered. If the site is not within an existing service area, or if the water purveyor does allow a new Group A water system within their jurisdiction, then the Washington State Department of Health may accept an application. This application must include information describing how rainwater offers comparable supply and quality as other available water supply options such as a well, public water supply or surface water intake. Rainwater is only considered as a primary water source if other water sources are considered unfeasible. Rainwater is then considered a surface

water source and required to be treated in the same way as river or lake sources that may contain polluted runoff from roadways, industry, agriculture and other land uses. It is also required to carry a disinfection residual, meaning it needs to be chlorinated. Under the Living Building Challenge, chlorine is considered a forbidden Red List chemical. (The Red List is an Imperative of the Materials Petal, explained in more detail beginning on page 125).

In order for Bertschi students to be allowed to drink the rain they have captured, the school would need to be reclassified as a new Group A water system. This redesign option would trigger the need to have a full-time staff member who could take daily samples of the treated rainwater on-site and then have those independently verified. Since Bertschi School's primary focus is operating as a school, this is not a feasible task.

Although we knew going into the Living Building project that potable water treatment would be an issue in this jurisdiction, we pursued it at length. Team members engaged city, county and state regulators through numerous meetings and symposia because we believe in the decentralized water treatment the Challenge supports. While there were individuals in each of

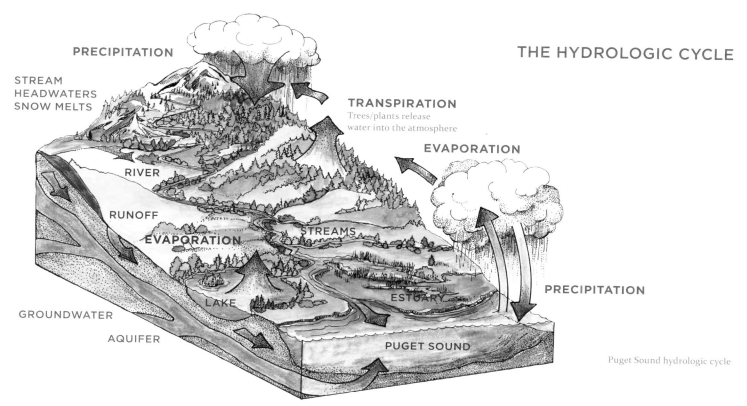

PRECIPITATION

STREAM
HEADWATERS
SNOW MELTS

TRANSPIRATION
Trees/plants release
water into the atmosphere

EVAPORATION

RIVER

RUNOFF

EVAPORATION

STREAMS

PRECIPITATION

LAKE

ESTUARY

GROUNDWATER

AQUIFER

PUGET SOUND

Puget Sound hydrologic cycle

these agencies who supported our intent, it was clear that they were not in a position to set a precedent with our system. Colleen believes that for these standards to change, several advancements would need to be made including, "updated guidance and regulations based on a better understanding of what types of contaminants, and in what concentrations, exist on our roofs; a performance-based treatment requirement for obtaining water quality benchmarks; a more appropriate sampling and testing protocol; and higher confidence in predictable, successful maintenance and operations tasks."

So, even facing these immense regulatory hurdles that have been in place for years, Bertschi School had the foresight to install the entire system needed to treat rainwater. The system consists of several filters. Water first flows through a five micron cartridge filter, then an ultraviolet disinfection system and finally through a .5 micron block carbon filter. Since this system is not permitted for use, the city required the project team to provide an air gap and a shut-off valve. At this time, the system is functional and has been used for testing to help promote decentralized rainwater treatment systems.

IMPERATIVE:
ECOLOGICAL WATER FLOW

The second and most difficult part of the Water Petal is the Ecological Water Flow Imperative. This Imperative involves managing all water used on-site including grey, black and stormwater.

It is one thing to collect and store the water a particular building might need in the course of a year but it is significantly more difficult to manage the treatment of all water on-site. This is what the Ecological Water Flow Imperative asks projects to accomplish. For Bertschi, this is one example of an Imperative that the tight urban site makes difficult to achieve. In our project, the treatment of grey- and blackwater on-site went through several evolutions. Eventually, as with other features of the building, the Bertschi students would prove to have the answer in their wish list.

81

WEST ECOHOUSE SECTION

1. North, insulated curtain wall glazing provides daylighting and natural ventilation

2. Skylights provide additional toplighting for the green wall

3. Greywater filter tanks remove large particulate matter before sending to green wall

4. Green wall treats all grey water on-site through closed-loop evapotranspiration

5. Vacuum flush toilet

6. Composting units (2) treat all blackwater on-site

7. Portable water treatment system (wall mounted) including micron filters and UV light for disinfection

8. Radiant floor hybrid hot water heater

9. Moss mat green roof

10. 12x12 wood framed, cellulose insulated walls

11. SIPS panel roof

12. Porous concrete outdoor classroom

1. Church building rain leader to cistern, exposed for education

2. Rain leader from classroom butterfly roof

3. Glass-covered interior runnel transports rain water to potable cistern

4. Potable water cistern

5. Potable tank hand pump for water appreciation

6. Energy Recovery Ventilator (ductwork omitted for clarity)

7. Operable curtain wall window for ventilation

©KMD Architects

83

The Water Petal: THE HYDROLOGIC CYCLE COMES TO LIFE

AN INTENTIONAL MOSS ROOF

When designing a building's water management system, the place to begin is with stormwater. In the case of the science building, all stormwater that falls on the site must be managed through natural means. The idea is to mimic the natural pre-development conditions of the site (the Cascade Forest).

No stormwater is allowed to enter city pipes to be managed off-site. However, in some jurisdictions like Seattle, it may be necessary to still make these connections but it is up to each individual project team to determine how to achieve this stipulation. Our team estimated that in a natural forested condition, about 40 percent of rainfall evapotranspires, 40 percent turns to runoff and 20 percent infiltrates to provide groundwater recharge. The Bertschi project uses approximately 40 percent of the average annual rainfall for water demands while the remaining 60 percent of the average annual rainfall either evapotranspires through the landscapes on-site or infiltrates into the native soils below.

The building is handling the water that falls on its site, including the building's roof and also some additional water from the church building next door. These 32,400 gallons of water from the church are used to help meet anticipated potable water needs. About 42,300 gallons are collected from the project site. The initial treatment for stormwater begins with our green roof system. A traditional green roof system consists of several layers of growth medium, root barriers, protection layers all over a roofing membrane and a building's roof structure. Depending on the type of plants to be grown on a particular green roof, the soil profiles can be from one to several inches thick. Plants can be very low profile or they can be heavily vegetated, taller varieties. Each system has its own benefits for certain amounts of water infiltration or the climate in which they are located.

At Bertschi, the science building is located on the north side of the church, which effectively provides no direct sunlight to the roof. This orientation makes it hard for most types of green roof

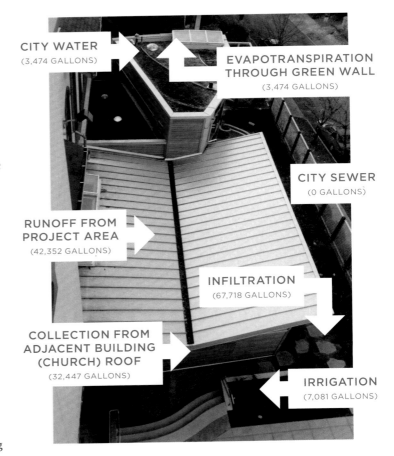

CITY WATER
(3,474 GALLONS)

EVAPOTRANSPIRATION THROUGH GREEN WALL
(3,474 GALLONS)

CITY SEWER
(0 GALLONS)

RUNOFF FROM PROJECT AREA
(42,352 GALLONS)

INFILTRATION
(67,718 GALLONS)

COLLECTION FROM ADJACENT BUILDING (CHURCH) ROOF
(32,447 GALLONS)

IRRIGATION
(7,081 GALLONS)

grasses and plants to survive. What does work well in the shade on the north side of a building in the Pacific Northwest is moss. Mark Sindell advised us that "mosses will thrive in the shady, northern exposure and can survive with no supplemental water during the dry summer months." In addition, the "use of mosses reinforces the use of quintessential Pacific Northwest plants, and provides yet another educational tool that connects young students to their native environment." Our system is the first intentional moss mat roof on the West Coast. Intentional is important here because in the Northwest, moss grows freely and easily. When first presenting this design feature, we had multiple Bertschi parents jokingly offer the moss from the roofs of their own homes. Another benefit to our system is that it is extremely low profile. The native mosses sit atop a water retention fleece and a root barrier, which create a very light system. This is the first stop for infiltrating rainwater. Any excess from the roof is sent to the irrigation cistern.

84

RAIN GARDEN

Managing stormwater on-site is an important ecological consideration because the goal is to return developed sites to their pre-development conditions. This process also reduces downstream impacts such as erosion and flooding while preventing pollutants from entering water bodies. In Washington State, the Department of Natural Resources finds that urban stormwater runoff and construction activities contribute to 16 percent of impaired or polluted streams, 10 percent of lakes and 13 percent of estuaries.[25] Bertschi School is located in what used to be the Cascade Forest from the mountain range that lies just to the east of Seattle. In the South Puget Sound area, where Bertschi is located, most urban watersheds are 20-40 percent covered with hard surfaces.[26]

The natural forested conditions for the project boundary were calculated to have historically produced an annual runoff volume of around 28,800 gallons for our specific site. This is important to note as downstream hydrologic patterns have historically been fed by this contribution of stormwater. Even the smallest amount of water in a watershed can have far-reaching implications on an entire ecosystem. For Bertschi, this fact is particularly important because of the school's location towards the top of a rather steep urban hillside. The water that is infiltrated on this site can have consequences to down slope homes and roads. In comparison, we have reduced the annual runoff volume from the forested condition by approximately 34 percent, which will aid in maintaining the downstream hydrology while mitigating the large storm volumes. Managing stormwater on-site naturally is even an important economic consideration. State studies have shown that it could "cost as much as $2.4 billion to build a stormwater system equivalent to that provided by forests converted to other uses in the last decade."[27]

All of the stormwater that falls on the Bertchi site (since we cannot use rainwater for potable use yet) eventually makes its way to the ethnobotanical rain garden. Here, rainwater either falls directly on it, overflows into it from any excess that

Porous concrete outdoor learning space

the cisterns can handle or is piped in from other parts of the campus. Designed to handle a 100-year storm, the rain garden consists of a minimum depth of 18" of compost amended soil containing course washed sand, pumice, spagnum peat, and a top layer of fine bark that filters out particulates, heavy metals, hydrocarbons and other pollutants before water infiltrates into the ground. In the first year of operation, the Bertschi rain garden infiltrated about 67,000 gallons of rainwater.

In addition to the rain garden, porous concrete pavement was also used throughout the site. This concrete, which acts like sand to allow water to filter through rather than run off, also filters sediment and particulates. Biological life that exists within the pavement section and the chipped rock that serves as a base just below the surface provides further filtration of hydrocarbons and other pollutants before rainwater is ultimately infiltrated back into the earth. These concrete hardscape spaces allow the students to have access to the garden during wet times while not compromising the site's ability to naturally infiltrate stormwater. To put the concept of stormwater runoff into a relevant perspective, consider this: the runoff from a one-acre meadow during a 1" rainstorm would fill a typical office to a depth of 2'8". If the meadow were paved, the runoff would fill six typical offices, floor to ceiling.[28]

25 Blanche Sobottke, ed. *Our Changing Nature: Natural Resource Trends in Washington State.* Rep. N.p.: n.p., n.d. 1998.
26 MacGregor, Barbara, and Blanche Sobottke, eds. *Changing Our Water Ways: Trends in Washington's Water System.* Rep. N.p.: n.p., n.d. Dec. 2000.
27 Ibid.

28 Ibid

Lower moss matt roof and solatube

86

A GREENHOUSE WHERE SOMETHING IS ALWAYS GROWING

The most widely accepted definition of greywater is any non-sewage water from sinks, showers, baths and washing machines. However, each jurisdiction may have a slightly different definition of what it considers to be grey. When we first began to investigate treatment of greywater on-site, we looked at using sub-surface discharge.

Sub-surface discharge means that we would pump our greywater outside the building and slowly discharge it just below the topsoil level where the ground would naturally infiltrate and filter the water back into the water table. This practice has been used around the world for years but really only works when there is sufficient site area. It is necessary to be able to discharge the water away from any uses that might allow building occupants to come into contact with the water or cause possible ground water contamination and be large enough to handle the amount of water being discharged. For the Bertschi site, we did not have this space. In the City of Seattle, special reviews and even state level permits from the health department are required to handle greywater in this manner. However, managing greywater on the interior of a building is permitted through the Plumbing Code which allows for more flexibility of reuse while maintaining adequate health protection. Our project could not afford the extra expense or time for a health department review of exterior water treatment. We needed to find a way to treat greywater inside the building. Our team talked about Living Machines (specifically designed rooms or large planters with plants and bacteria that naturally clean water). These systems are amazing and demonstrate the power that nature has to perform functions as complex as water treatment with common plants. Certain varieties of plants can completely treat black or sewage water in as little as four days. Although this is a time-tested method for treating water on-site, the Bertschi project did not have the indoor space, water demand or budget to warrant such a system. Once again, we needed a scale-appropriate treatment method.

Remembering the students' wish list, we found "a place where something is always growing." From the beginning, we wanted to include this great amenity to let the children learn in a plant-filled space and create, as Mark Sindell puts it, "the most expressive sustainable design feature and teaching tool for the project." But providing a room full of plants simply for aesthetics is just not completely sustainable. I thought about the Living Machines and the on-site constructed wetlands that so beautifully treat water and asked our team if a green wall would work for our project. At that time, the green wall idea had only been a small design feature to give the students access to indoor growing plants. We also looked at it for the large, curving exterior wall of the Ecohouse. But treating water forced the green wall to become a much bigger part of the project and gave it a variety of functions that were useful to the building and educational to the students.

Green walls are not a new concept but treating greywater with them is. Phytoremediation is the direct use of green plants and their associated microorganisms to stabilize or reduce contamination in soils, sludges, sediments, surface water or ground water.[29] The Bertschi system is rather simple in design but detailed in its execution. The plants are common and usually used as house plants. Schefflera aboricola luseane, brake fern, Xanadu philodendron and petite peace lily were all pre-grown off-site so that once delivered to Bertschi School they would be fully functional and ready to take greywater. The plants are held in a non-soil structural growth medium composed of coconut husk which reduces erosion and maintains plant longevity while also reducing maintenance. The plants and coconut husk are housed within one foot by one foot aluminum planter boxes. Each of these boxes is mounted on a metal support frame attached directly to the interior exposed concrete wall of the Ecohouse. Running throughout the entire framework of planter boxes is a series of irrigation lines that delivers the greywater from the science room's sinks through slow drips directly to the growth medium. The plants use the greywater as their irrigation water. Through their natural processes, the plants evapotranspire the greywater into the air. At times when sink water demand is reduced, like during summer recess, supplemental rainwater is used to irrigate. This portion of the irrigation system, along with fertilizer, is remotely controlled from the green wall manufacturer's office.

29 "Using Phytoremediation to Clean Up Sites." *EPA*. Environmental Protection Agency, n.d. Web. 14 Aug. 2013.

Aqua2 greywater filter box treats water before sending it to the green wall

The phytoremediation in Bertschi's wall is a completely closed process. This design means that no greywater has to leave the green wall system and in the first year of operations the nearly 200 square feet of plant-covered wall evapotranspired almost 3,500 gallons. Because of health regulations that do not allow greywater to be stored more than twenty-four hours in a commercial building, there is no storage tank for the greywater. Instead, water continues to cycle through the system until it is completely used by the plants. Any excess greywater that may not infiltrate during the first irrigation pass through the wall falls into a three-foot deep planter box just below the plants that contains a sandy compost amended soil. Once here, the water can be pumped back up through the plants until completely evapotranspired.

Before being sent to the green wall of plants for the final treatment, greywater is first sent directly from the sink drains to one of two Matala Aqua2Use greywater tanks. These tanks are comprised of several filter pads of various densities that get progressively smaller, each helping to filter our various particulates within the greywater such as hair, detergent clogs and small particles. One of these tanks is located directly under the sinks in the science room and the other is in the mechanical closet in the restroom. Greywater from the sinks and lavatory is gravity-fed to these tanks and then is automatically pumped to the green wall drip irrigation heads after it has been filtered. This process is essential so that these filtered particulates do not clog the small and sensitive green wall irrigation heads. This system is very low energy as water has a short distance to travel and the filtration process is rather simple, making it ideal for our net zero water and net zero energy needs.

The evapotranspiration process mimicked in Bertschi's green wall is performed every day, right here in Puget Sound. "Of the vast amount of water trapped by plants, only one-fifth stays in the bodies of plants. The remaining four-fifths, ever on the move, is called the water of evapotranpiration. Water lost to the atmosphere from plants and adjacent soil is transformed by the energy of the sun into its gaseous form, water vapor. Of the solar energy reaching vegetation, 40 percent effectively enters the machinery of the plant body, there to be unevenly divided between a minuscule allotment of energy to photosynthesis and a lion's share of the energy to speed water on its way from soil through the plant, back to the atmosphere. The initial phase of evapotranspiration is simply the loss of water vapor from leaf and other porous plant surfaces; an equivalent volume is replaced in the so-called transpirational stream: countless capillary thread of liquid water in the tubular conducting system (xylem cells) of roots, trunks, twigs and leaves, as well as in the porous microscopic meshwork of cellulose cell walls of the entire plant. The major control is by the leaf, a marvelous contrived "sandwich" of photosynthesthic, conductive, storage, protective, and ventilation tissues. Ventilation is the prime function of the lower epidermis of a leaf, with its many regularly spaced pores (stomates).[30]

Evapotranspiration is a critical process that occurs in vegetation throughout the world. Interestingly, scientists have actually been able to quantify the amount of water that trees evapotranspire through an experiment performed in the Cedar River Watershed near Seattle. Here, an ingenious device was created and installed under a 92-foot tall Douglas fir to effectively weigh the amount of water to precise accuracy down to the gram of water weight. Through this measurement, data was extrapolated to determine the annual water loss by evapotranspiration

30 Kruckeberg, Arthur R. *The Natural History of Puget Sound Country.* Seattle: University of Washington, 1991. Print.

from one acre of second-growth Douglas fir is around 546,405 gallons.[31] This amazing natural process is now miniaturized and incorporated into the Bertschi students' classroom.

Of course, designing this first-of-its-kind wall was not a simple task. GGLO spent considerable time working to find the most appropriate plant species to work with the variable conditions because the plants needed to not only survive, but thrive. First, the Ecohouse is intentionally kept much cooler than the remaining science building. This energy saving strategy allows the room to save on heating energy — a strategy that will play into the Net Zero Energy Imperative. In addition to being a cool room that often remains in the 50F range during the winter, the Ecohouse does not receive direct sunlight and the plants are almost constantly in damp conditions with the greywater. But, as the design for the green wall progressed, the manufacturer began to have concerns about the amount of natural light that would reach the wall. To alleviate these concerns, a system of metal halide lights on a track fixture was meticulously designed to be added to the wall. To help with this, GGLO worked closely with the University of Washington's Lighting Design Lab to perform careful studies of the foot-candle light distribution on the wall. The metal halide bulbs have the correct spectrum of light to support plant growth. The lighting system is managed by a complex system of controls, including an astronomical clock and daylight sensors that switch each light on and off, on different phases, according to where and when light is needed on specific parts of the wall.

Since its installation, the wall has performed well. At only one time was there an issue with a single plant species that did not grow well. The brake fern plants were promptly replaced with a species that was already doing well on the wall and since then, everything has been thriving. At times, beautiful blooms are present on the wall. Maintenance for the wall occurs monthly with a local landscaping company that performs trimming and looks for possible root diseases and monitors water levels.

31 Ibid.

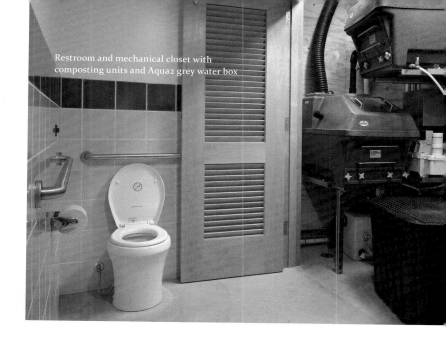

Restroom and mechanical closet with composting units and Aqua2 grey water box

COMPOSTING TOILET

The developed world uses potable water to flush its defecation and urination and there are better ways to address human waste management. Bertschi School has a much more reasonable and ecologically-minded solution for its waste management.

Perhaps one of the most controversial and surprisingly exciting features of the Living Building is the blackwater, or sewage-treating composting toilet. The goal here, in terms of ecological practices, is to decentralize the water treatment process so that each site becomes responsible for managing the wastewater that is created. And when we begin to think in this decentralized manner and realize the growing water issues on the planet, we begin to re-imagine what is actually considered waste. In a net zero water building, there is no wastewater, no matter the color classification of grey, black, yellow or brown water. Colleen reminds us that, "all water is a resource as are the nutrients and life within it."

Decentralizing the water treatment process can not only save water that may be lost during the transport or treatment process due to failing infrastructure and the often miles of pipe water must travel through to a municipal water treatment facility, but it also saves energy. However, a water-independent building may not necessarily

89

1. Outside Air/Oxygen Enters

2. Air is Heated

3. Heated Air forced down

4. Automatic six-way Aeration™

5. Evaporation

6. Composting

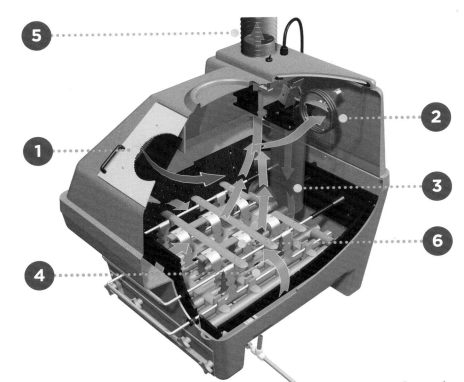

be right in all instances. A connection to the municipal system might be necessary for emergency back-up or supply for fire suppression.

The idea of a composting toilet might not sit well with many clients and so our team felt an understandable nervousness knowing we would need to present this option to Bertschi School. However, we were completely surprised to find the school more than accepting of our proposal. In fact, the Board told us they have been considering this type of fixture for years and that the facilities committee and many parents have already been supportive of the idea. We were relieved knowing that acceptance is one of the most difficult aspects of composting toilet implementation. Our team also felt strongly about the educational opportunities of such a design. "I believe by exposing them to the composting toilet at this age," says Stacy, "it has the potential to change how they think about waste and waste management as they become adults." With support from the school and parent community, we began to design the system.

Our initial design for treating blackwater looked at a variety of options. As with greywater, constructed wetlands and Living Machines have been successfully used to treat this water on-site in other instances. But we once again ran into the issues of limited

space for these options. Also, with the small daily use of around fifty students per day, we did not have the high demand that would necessitate a large Living Machine, for example. Looking to treat a relatively small amount of water and perform the entire process indoors led us to a composting toilet system for "simplicity and nutrient reuse," says Colleen. Currently, there are several different models on the market for composting toilets. Our team, led by 2020 Engineering as experts in the water treatment area, began to focus on a unit called the Phoenix Composting Toilet. As we began to design around this system, we found some design issues. This particular system would require the installation of a basement solely for the unit as it must sit directly below the water closet (toilet). In addition, this basement room would need to be heated in order to provide the optimal operating temperature for the unit to properly compost. After further investigation we determined that the added site disturbance and expense to excavate a basement along with the added energy required to heat the space was not in the best interest of the Challenge-specific goals for the project. We chose to find a more suitable, low-impact alternative.

While we would still incorpote a composting toilet, we moved to a simpler and more compact unit. The Envirolet VF750 would allow our design to be completely contained above ground in a mechanical closet located inside the restroom. This revolution would save us from excavating a basement and heating an additional space. Coupled with a standard vacuum flush toilet that can be found on any commercial airplane or boat, the entire unit is significantly smaller than the Phoenix. Since it is important to be safe when it comes to waste, we installed two of the grey-box units from Envirolet. Both performed the same function but doubled our capacity. Like most composting toilets, the functions are very simple. Waste is sucked through the vacuum hose after being flushed with about .2 liters of rainwater and distributed to one of the two grey compost boxes.

Here, it settles to the bottom of the unit and mixes with specific compost accelerator additives, beginning the process of breaking down the waste through aeration and microbe activity. Human waste consists of a large percentage of liquid waste, so one of the most important parts of the compost process is evaporation. The units contain small heaters and along with a vent fan to draw exhaust through the roof vent stack so that the waste is desiccated. This process dramatically reduces the overall volume of the waste in its initial form, allowing greater storage capacity than might be expected. Envirolet advertises that compost from this unit will only need to be emptied about every six months depending on usage. For Bertschi, in the first year of operation, they have only had to empty once. The compost is used as plant fertilizer for ornamental plants on campus only. No compost is distributed in the edible portions of the garden to safeguard against ingesting any trace pharmaceutical remnants carried through the waste stream.

Although the Envirolet system is relatively straightforward, it has taken the school considerable effort to optimize its use. When blackwater treatment is decentralized, the maintenance portion of that process is as well. At Bertschi, there are no teams of engineers and facilities experts handling the waste treatment process at a distant water treatment plant. Instead, this work has been transferred to the facilities department at the school. Because of this, there has been a great deal of time spent determining the exact amount of water required for flushing, procedures for when to operate the compost heaters and fine-tuning of other systems. Ideally, we would have been able to use a gravity system, which would require less water for flushing, as well as a urine diversion toilet, which would have created a higher quality fertilizer by separating waste.

Overall, the entire net zero water system presented a great deal of challenges even for this small building in what is thought of as a water-rich ecosystem of the Pacific Northwest. Predicting both weather and human behavior is an integral part to designing this system but this is, of course, inherently difficult. Also, there is currently very little data regarding the systems used at Bertschi including greywater production, evapotranspiration rates and compost leachate production, to name a few.

While in recent years, there has been much attention focused on the energy use of buildings, water use is just as important. The declining amounts of fresh water on the planet is a tremendous problem for all living things. Wasting water has far-reaching and dramatic consequences visible around the globe. The old-fashioned hand-operated water pump located in the Ecohouse was installed just to bring awareness to these issues. The World Health Organization reports in 2013 that 2.5 billion people lack any improved sanitation facilities and 768 million people are without access to an improved drinking water source.[32] Many of these people must walk long distances each day just to reach a source of water that can be considered potable. Obviously, in advanced countries, we have the privilege of having potable water delivered — almost effortlessly — to our fixtures right in our home. We do not have to work for this water, we do not walk miles on a daily basis and then have to carry this water home on our backs. We do not have to wonder if our children's lives are at risk for drinking the water they have collected. Instead, we simply pull, or twist, or wave our hands by a faucet and clean water is delivered. Not everyone in the world has this luxury. The idea with the hand pump at Bertschi is that students have to think about how they get their water. They must put a little effort into extracting water from the Ecohouse cistern using the pump. Through classroom lessons, they even go a bit further and strap on water-filled containers like backpacks and walk around campus to gain some understanding of what so many in the world must overcome to meet basic needs. Conserving and reusing water as the Bertschi Living Building does is certainly a major improvement that is necessary for the built environment. But education of these issues and water solutions can be just as significant for future generations.

32 *Progress on Sanitation and Drinking Water: 2013 Update.* Rep. France: WHO, 2013. Web.

THE ENERGY PETAL

Learning to Conserve and Generate

93

SUMMARY OF THE LIVING BUILDING CHALLENGE VERSION 2.0 NET ZERO ENERGY PETAL

Petal Intent

The intent of this Petal is to signal a new age of design, wherein the built environment relies solely on renewable forms of energy and operates year-round in a pollution-free manner. In addition, it aims to prioritize reduction and optimization before technological solutions are applied to eliminate wasteful spending – of energy, resources and dollars.

Petal Imperative

• Net Zero Energy

94

IMPERATIVE:
NET ZERO ENERGY

Philosopher Max Weber says change comes excruciatingly slow to those who want it. On November 30, 2012, the Bertschi Living Building reached net zero energy. After nineteen months of faithfully tracking the school's energy use and production, seven months longer than the required and anticipated LBC 12-months, the team breathed a collective sigh of relief. So many people were watching, from Bertschi students and their parents who helped fund the project to people across the world interested in the Living Building. Net zero energy was indeed possible in Seattle.

There are several ways to think about net zero energy, and a number of ways to achieve and measure it.

- Net Zero Site Energy: A site (zero energy building) ZEB produces at least as much energy as it uses in a year, when accounted for at the site.

- Net Zero Source Energy: A source ZEB produces at least as much energy as it uses in a year, when accounted for at the source. Source energy refers to the primary energy used to generate and deliver the energy to the site.

- Net Zero Energy Costs: In a cost ZEB, the amount of money the utility pays the building owner for the energy the building exports to the grid is at least equal to the amount the owner pays the utility for the energy services and energy used over the year.

- Net Zero Energy Emissions: A net zero emissions building produces at least as much emissions-free renewable energy as it uses from emissions-producing energy sources.[33]

33 Torcellini, Paul, Shanti Pless, and Michael Deru. *Zero Energy Buildings: A Critical Look at the Definition.* Rep. N.p.: National Renewable Energy Laboratory, 2006. Print.

95

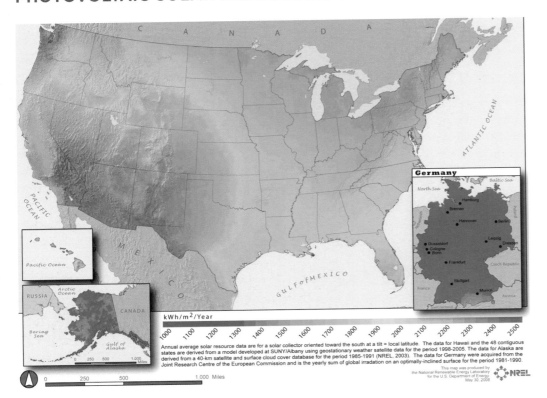

kWh/m²/Year

Annual average solar resource data are for a solar collector oriented toward the south at a tilt = local latitude. The data for Hawaii and the 48 contiguous states are derived from a model developed at SUNY/Albany using geostationary weather satellite data for the period 1998-2005. The data for Alaska are derived from a 40-km satellite and surface cloud cover database for the period 1985-1991 (NREL, 2003). The data for Germany were acquired from the Joint Research Centre of the European Commission and is the yearly sum of global irradation on an optimally-inclined surface for the period 1981-1990.

This map was produced by the National Renewable Energy Laboratory for the U.S. Department of Energy
May 30, 2008

RENEWABLE ENERGY FROM THE SUN

Often there is question of whether photovoltaic (PV) panels will work well in the generally cloudy Seattle climate. This doubt is a common misconception in Seattle, as the solar insolation, or the radiation energy from the sun that can be converted into electricity, is equal to or greater than what Germany receives. Continuing into 2014, Germany has long been considered the global solar leader with the most installed PV capacity.[34]

The Bertschi School achieves net zero energy through Net Zero Energy costs with a grid-tied design, meaning that although PVs are installed on-site, the building is still connected to the city utility grid. The process involved is called net metering, wherein a building's electric meter spins backwards to record the positive energy produced through PVs that is being fed back into the utility grid. The process of determining net zero is then the result of a simple math calculation: the building must produce at least as much energy as it has used over a year's time. This design works well for places like Seattle where a much greater amount of solar energy can be produced during the summer months than in the winter months.

There are several advantages to using a PV system to achieve Bertschi's energy independence. From an operations and maintenance standpoint, PVs offer a straightforward system requiring very little maintenance over their lifespan. This system also allows for net metering without having to store

34 Masson, Gaetan. *Global Market Outlook for Photovoltaics* 2013-2017. Rep. Ed. Craig Winneker. European Photovoltaic Industry Association, May 2013. Web.

energy in batteries on-site and no green house gases are created from their use. (Another option the design team investigated, although only to supplement a primary PV system, was wind energy. The team found that wind patterns in this urban environment were too variable and the scale of the system was not appropriate for the mostly residential neighborhood.)

The team performed extensive research on finding the right PV system from a variety of PV panels available on the market, each with varying efficiencies and capacities. Choosing the right one meant balancing panel capacity with available roof area and, of course, cost. As the team continued to investigate options, in May 2010 the project received one of the first and most influential manufacturer contributions. Interested in a project aiming to achieve Living Building Challenge certification, a local supplier, West Seattle Natural Energy, had bid on the project to provide PVs. In addition to donating some of their products and services, the company proposed a PV panel that was coupled with a microinverter. In a conventional solar panel system, energy from the PV panel is routed through wiring to a single inverter where the electric current produced through the sun's energy is converted from AC to DC so that it can be used to power various pieces of equipment in a building. But a microinverter system operates differently and converts the current immediately at the PV panel on the roof, resulting in a much more efficient system. (At the Bertschi site, the team calculated there would have been a line loss of approximately 18 percent of the electricity that the solar panels produced if the conventional inverter was used.) In additon the microinverter system allows greater monitoring of the PV system and, as a bonus also allows the Bertschi students to see the processes working to power their building.

The site of the new science building, located on the north side of the church building, presented some difficulties with solar access. The roof of the building would be shaded almost the entire year, and with a 215 watt panel that is only 14 percent efficient, direct sun was needed to make a net zero PV system a viable option. To achieve solar access, the team used the Challenge concept of scale jumping. Scale jumping allows projects to work outside of the site boundary to achieve the intent of an Imperative. Specifically for Bertschi, this allowed us to place our PV panels on the south-facing, unobstructed roof of the adjacent church building. This alternative added distance from the PV panels to the building made an even greater case for avoiding the line loss and using the efficient microinverter system.

Workers install the first PV panels

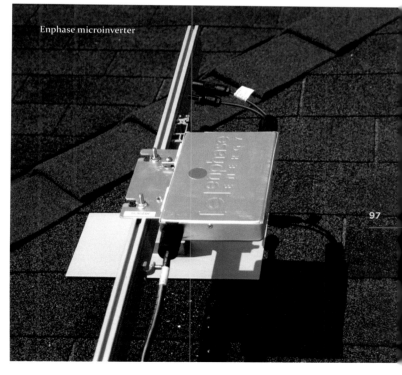

Enphase microinverter

97

ENERGY USE ASSESSMENT

When the team began the Bertschi project, net zero energy was one of the first major goals we looked to achieve. Building energy use affects, or is affected by, almost every process in a building. Therefore, it was critical that all project team members follow an integrated, collaborative, research and design process.

The first step in designing for a building's energy use is to assess current owner processes, needs and actual energy consumption. Through detailed discussions and analysis with science specialist Julie Blystadt, the team sought to understand the school's needs. From the outset the team's goal was always to design a healthy and efficient Living Building that did not limit the school's curriculum. This analysis process helped identify what classroom functions were necessary and where energy reduction could be achieved.

"We looked for the demands that were necessary for the building but that could be influenced by our design, such as heating and ventilation. We knew that the scale of this project made some of the traditional high-efficiency systems impractical. In the end we decided to put together a system that was appropriate both in scale and sophistication, did not rely on high-end components, and most importantly, would meet the specific needs of the classroom."

NATHAN MILLER
Energy Analyst and
Mechanical Engineer, Rushing

Green wall supplementary lighting

98

LIVING BUILDING EDUCATION

The weather barrier is an important component of an efficient envelope

DESIGNING THE ENVELOPE

Once the energy requirements of the science building were determined, the next step was designing an efficient building envelope. The envelope, which includes the exterior skin (walls), roof and floor of the building, is critical in supporting an energy-efficient building by reducing the impacts of a particular climate on human comfort. Acknowledging that the design for the building would consist of a wood structure and framing to match the Northwest architectural style, the team needed to determine the details.

For the envelope, the team chose a 2x12 wood stud wall rather than more standard 2x4 wall. The greater thickness allows for an increase in the amount of insulation in the wall cavity, and creates a more thermally efficient envelope. Calculating the heat and moisture transport through the various materials of wall design helped to determine the necessary thicknesses and even the order of materials within the insulated wall assembly. The same approach was applied to the roof assembly. Here, the team also wanted to simplify the structure because of the small space and the desire to

use the least amount of materials possible. This goal led to the decision to use structurally insulated panels (SIPs) for the roof. Bertschi structural engineer Jack Wiggens explains that SIPs were chosen because they would provide the highest insulation-to-material ratio for the relatively simple roof form of the project. They arrive on-site preassembled and properly sized, thus saving construction time and greatly reducing material waste. A life cycle analysis of these locally manufactured SIPs show energy savings and reduced emissions when compared to traditional stick framing systems.

"The building envelope is the portion that separates the uncontrolled outdoor environment from the indoor controlled environment. A properly designed building envelope will control the movement of heat, air, water and water vapor across the envelope, which makes it possible for the other systems (like the radiant floor heating and natural ventilation) to control the indoor environment for occupant health and comfort with minimal addition of energy."

MEDGAR MARCEAU
Building Envelop Consultant, Morrison Hershfield

"We knew going in that the scale of this project made some of the traditional high-efficiency systems impractical. It simply wasn't in the budget to install a ground-source heat pump system to serve a single classroom. In the end we decided to put together a system that was appropriate in scale and sophistication, didn't rely on high-end components, and most importantly, would meet the specific needs of the classroom."

NATHAN MILLER
Energy Analyst and Mechanical Engineer, Rushing

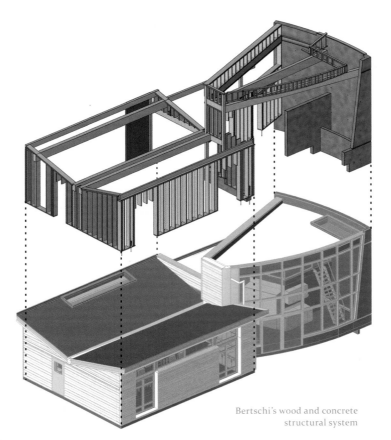

Bertschi's wood and concrete structural system

Glazing is another important consideration for building efficiency. Any decision to maximize the amount of windows to allow in daylight, fresh air and provide views comes at an efficiency cost because glass is not as insulative as a solid wall can be. For Bertschi, the team chose glass with a 0.25 u-value (u-value is the measure of heat loss in an element and u-values close to zero indicate that a material is more insulating). The choice of a glass with a low u-value that also allowed 70 percent of visible light through helped to keep the envelope thermally efficient while satisfying occupants with the windows and natural light they desired.

Project team members worked diligently to reduce thermal bridging throughout the envelope. Thermal bridging occurs when thermal conduction passes through building materials from the exterior to the interior. An example of this would be the cold outside air coming into contact with a window frame. Through thermal bridging, the cold is transferred through the frame to the building interior. This bridging is undesirable because even with a well-insulated envelope, the exterior thermal conditions can transfer directly into the building interior, greatly reducing the effectiveness of a building's ability to protect against the climate. One of the ways the design team chose to help reduce thermal bridging was to provide insulation where the floor slab and exterior wall meet.

The final designed envelope consists of a SIP roof of R-31 insulation sandwiched between OSB for a total u-factor of 0.030 Btu/hr·ft2·°F, a wall assembly of R-48 blown-in insulation between 2x12 wood studs with a cedar siding rain screen system for a total u-factor of .027 Btu/hr·ft2·°F. The floor consists of a 4-inch concrete slab with a 3-inch concrete topping slab all over under slab R-11 rigid insulation.

The SIPs roof being installed

100

The red hydronic radiant floor tubes waiting to be covered in concrete

"This system provides a very comfortable environment but doesn't require the fan energy of a traditional forced-air system. Radiant floors also pair very nicely with our heating system, an air-to-water heat pump, because they are more efficient when they are not trying to produce high water temperatures. A forced-air system might require 180°F hot water, but the radiant floor works well with 100°F hot water."

NATHAN MILLER
Energy Analyst and Mechanical Engineer, Rushing

CHOOSING BUILDING SYSTEMS

After the building envelope was designed to be as efficient as possible, the next step was to select the most appropriate and efficient building systems. Armed with the knowledge that heating typically accounts for the largest energy use in buildings in the Pacific Northwest, the team needed to determine what functions would be required from the building's mechanical system. The mild, maritime climate of the Cascadia region eliminated the need for mechanical cooling. A building designed to use cross or stack ventilation with a low rate of heat gain can meet its cooling load with daytime natural ventilation all but 3.5 days of the year in Seattle.[35] This knowledge played an important part in reducing our energy budget because the mechanical system would only need to be used for heating, not cooling.

During the course of the building systems investigations some design work and components for a geothermal system were offered as donations. However, the team decided that although it would be great to have a sophisticated and efficient system, the added materials and site disturbance were not consistent with the values of the Living Building Challenge. Balancing the project's budget with its net zero energy goals was exacting. For example, although selection of a lower cost system might have first cost benefits, there could possibly be a

sacrifice in energy efficiency with a lower performing system and consequently forcing an increase in the PV system budget.

The goal was to have a simple and efficient system for heating, which led the team to decide on a hydronic radiant floor. An air-to-water heat pump located in the mezzanine of Ecohouse provides this hot water to the radiant floor. The heat pump mode extracts heat from the Ecohouse by recovering built-up heat from solar gain, electric lighting and the warm student bodies. Moreover, it pulls moisture out of the air and puts it back into the green wall cycle and rejects cold air, blowing it toward the relief vent.

Coupled with our radiant flooring, the classroom also has high ventilation air requirements, which account for the building's largest heating load. While this ventilation is beneficial in a learning environment from a healthy air perspective, there is a significant energy penalty to heat all of this outside air being brought in for ventilation. The solution for this conundrum is a unit called an energy recovery ventilator, or ERV. The ERV is a heat-exchanger that heats incoming fresh air by transferring heat from the exhausting stale air inside the building and dumping the exhaust air while losing the heat that goes with it. Utilizing this process there is a savings of about two-thirds of the heating load from the outside air and the remaining one-third coming from a small in-line electric coil that tempers the air to a 'neutral' 65-70° F."

35 Brown, G.Z., Jeff Kline, Gina Livingston, Dale Northcutt, and Emily Wright. Natural Ventilation in Northwest Buildings. Eugene: University of Oregon, 2004. Print.

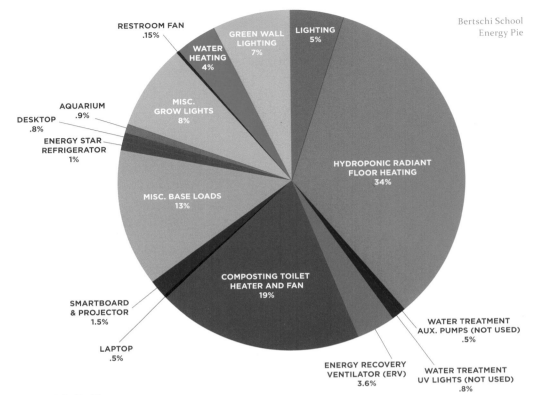

"The combination of a thermally efficient envelope combined with an energy recovery ventilation system was the key. These two measures minimize the heating load in the space, which allowed us to simplify the heating system."

NATHAN MILLER
Energy Analyst and
Mechanical Engineer, Rushing

Pie chart labels: RESTROOM FAN .15%, WATER HEATING 4%, GREEN WALL LIGHTING 7%, LIGHTING 5%, MISC. GROW LIGHTS 8%, AQUARIUM .9%, DESKTOP .8%, ENERGY STAR REFRIGERATOR 1%, HYDROPONIC RADIANT FLOOR HEATING 34%, MISC. BASE LOADS 13%, SMARTBOARD & PROJECTOR 1.5%, LAPTOP .5%, COMPOSTING TOILET HEATER AND FAN 19%, WATER TREATMENT AUX. PUMPS (NOT USED) .5%, ENERGY RECOVERY VENTILATOR (ERV) 3.6%, WATER TREATMENT UV LIGHTS (NOT USED) .8%

ENERGY MODELING

Once building design and system selection begins to progress on a project, one of the most significant first steps is to complete an energy model. An energy model is a virtual simulation of a building's operation taking into account climate, building orientation and shape along with building envelope and building systems. These simulation tools help design teams to predict what the effects of each of these variables has on a building's performance and, ultimately, its energy use. Energy models are essential for the design of most building types, especially net zero energy buildings.

While most energy models are completed with software that essentially builds a virtual model of a building, the design team used a spreadsheet for Bertschi. This method of modeling allows the team to maintain "a very fine level of detail regarding the end-uses of our energy," says Nathan Miller. However, he goes on to explain that, "the main drawback to this approach is that we lose some of the interactive effects of the systems that you see in an energy model, but we felt it would result in more conservative results if anything." A large portion of this modeling included specific hour-by-hour heating load

calculation, based on historic weather data, because that was the most complicated and largest energy end-use.

The data provided by the energy model helped us to estimate the total capacity needed for the PV system. From there, Miller and his team used the National Renewable Energy Labs (NREL) PV Watts program to estimate the sizing and output of the PV system the Bertschi building would need. This program uses the most recent thirty years of meteorological data, specifically solar irradiance, to predict how much energy a PV system might produce in a particular area.

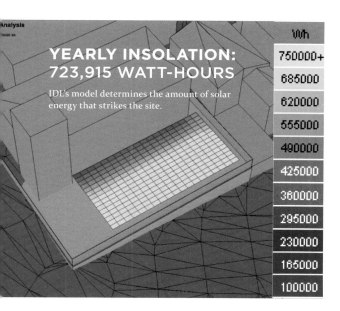

**YEARLY INSOLATION:
723,915 WATT-HOURS**

IDL's model determines the amount of solar
energy that strikes the site.

Wh
750000+
685000
620000
555000
490000
425000
360000
295000
230000
165000
100000

Analysis

DAYLIGHT STUDY

IDL's daylight model shows the distribution
of natural light in the classroom.

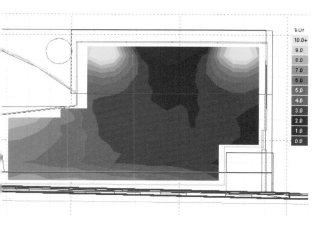

%UF

| 10.0+ |
| 9.0 |
| 8.0 |
| 7.0 |
| 6.0 |
| 5.0 |
| 4.0 |
| 3.0 |
| 2.0 |
| 1.0 |
| 0.0 |

"It's that empowerment and understanding if we have solar
panels and we measure the energy on a weekly basis and
we know we are net zero energy, we can do it; empowering
the children that they actually can make a difference."

BRIGITTE BERTSCHI
Head of Bertschi School

DAYLIGHTING

In the initial planning stages of the building team members knew that
daylighting would be a significant design feature to reduce energy use
and, most importantly, to provide optimal human comfort. Particularly in
educational environments, the benefits of daylighting have been shown to
improve test scores, reduce absenteeism and simply provide a more enjoyable
environment. Once again, the north side location of the building would add
some difficulty to designing a naturally lit classroom. To help with daylighting
design, the team enlisted the services of the Seattle Integrated Design
Lab (IDL). Supported by the University of Washington, this lab provides
a range of expert daylighting simulation and verification information.

With the existing church buildings and surrounding trees, the Living
Building site receives 10,800 lux of average overcast solar energy for the year
with the yearly insolation equaling 723,915 watt-hours. Interestingly, team
members also determined that the existing white-colored building across
Lynn Street to the north was helping to reflect some daylighting back to the
Bertschi site. However, the site only receives direct sunlight during summer
months while the remainder of the year sees predominantly overcast light.

Working through various side and toplighting design options, the team
finished with a design that provides a 4.7 percent average daylight factor.
Our target amount was to have a daylight factor of at least 3. Daylight
factor (DF) is a measure of overcast light that represents the amount of
illumination available indoors relative to the illumination present outdoors.

Overall, the IDL helped the design team create a building that provided
a well daylit space for students and plants while helping to reduce the
need for electric lighting. Electric lighting was finalized at .99 watts
per square foot for a 7 percent reduction from code. Coupled with
the use of daylight and occupancy sensors to reduce the electric
lighting that is needed, the daylighting design for the building helps
to reduce one of the biggest demands on total energy use: lighting.

103

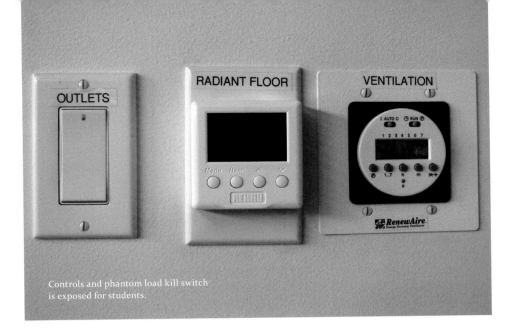

Controls and phantom load kill switch is exposed for students.

"Like any building, it needs to be lived in. You have to get used to it. You need to understand it. This building perhaps more than any other. I think that level of awareness is probably one of the most valuable things that anybody can get out of the Challenge."

STAN RICHARDSON
Director of Campus Planning,
Bertschi School

PLUG LOADS AND PHANTOM LOADS

For years, plug loads were an often overlooked component of building energy use. Recent data is showing that plug loads are responsible for a large portion of a building's energy. In fact, the NREL reports that up to 28 percent of energy use in office buildings can be attributed just to plug loads.[36]

Plug loads are defined as energy consumed by any electronic device plugged into an outlet. The other component of plug loads is what is called a phantom load which occurs when any plugged in electronic device draws power in standby mode or when turned off. These small trickles of energy constantly feeding a device can add up to a significant amount of waste. Plug loads must be accounted for in building energy modeling, especially when trying to reach net zero energy. And because plug loads are largely based on occupant behavior, efforts must be taken to anticipate and manage these electrical draws.

At Bertschi, the majority of the outlets in the room were set into a time clock tied to the main electrical panel. This system shuts off power from the panel to the outlets at the end of each day, effectively eliminating any phantom loads. Additionally, there is a wall switch that allows the teacher to

perform the same function and switch off power to these outlets. Students are taught the importance of eliminating plug loads and encouraged not to leave electronics plugged in when not in use. [36]

A net zero building requires efficiency at every point. It demands solutions that may change operations from business as usual. One of these changes happens when portions of the building are shut down when not in use. For the school, this occurred with turning heat, lights and other equipment off in rooms not in use. During the summer recess, the school ensured that as many of the building's systems as possible were turned off. This selective shutdown process extended to school holidays throughout the year. This energy reduction strategy is actually what should be followed in homes and commercial buildings everywhere.

36 Metzger, Ian, Alicen Kandt, and Otto VanGeet. *Plug Load Behavioral Change Demonstration Project*. Tech. Golden: NREL, 2011. Web.

104

ACTUAL ENERGY USE

In order for a building to be certified as a Living Building, the Challenge requires that it meets each of the twenty Imperatives after a one-year period of occupancy. The Bertschi team decided to begin its year clock not on the day of the grand opening, but nearly two months later — after the team had taken time to tune the building.

Bertschi's facilities staff learned how the equipment throughout the building worked, the proper timing for the lights and best temperature set points for the spaces. There were a few things that did not work properly during this time, like a wall switch for one of the Ecohouse lights and a failed pump in the irrigation cistern that ran continually. All of these performance issues took time to identify and correct. Each glitch, no matter how seemingly small, wasted energy and the team wanted to ensure the building was performing optimally before the Challenge's one-year clock began.

As the first year was underway, the design team and students watched the building's energy consumption very closely. Students took weekly readings of both the energy use and power production from the PVs. But as the months rolled by, the design team began to see that the building was not performing to the level it had expected so it tried to isolate each of the energy uses and monitor their performance. What began to emerge was significant and unexpected energy use from two major components, both heating related. Firstly, the heaters within the composting toilet units were running continually and drawing nearly 1100 watts. The function of the heaters is essential to ensuring the proper evaporation of the waste to achieve compost. After a great deal of experimentation and work with the manufacturer, the school found the best setting to reduce the continual heavy energy draw while still performing the appropriate evaporation. Secondly, the heat pump, or hybrid hot water heater that heats the radiant floor, was not performing as efficiently as anticipated. This problem resulted from a combination of the unit not being as efficient as anticipated and its location in an unheated space — the Ecohouse. This combination prevented the heat pump from withdrawing as much warm air surrounding the unit as was hoped when operating in efficiency mode. Instead, this air-to-water heat pump is required to switch to electric-resistance mode more frequently, which drives up the energy use.

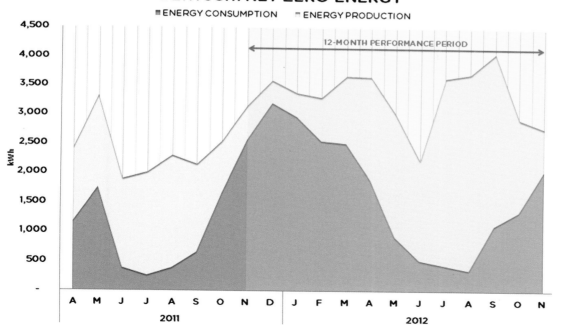

BERTSCHI NET ZERO ENERGY

■ ENERGY CONSUMPTION □ ENERGY PRODUCTION

12-MONTH PERFORMANCE PERIOD

kWh

4,500
4,000
3,500
3,000
2,500
2,000
1,500
1,000
500
-

A M J J A S O N D | J F M A M J J A S O N

2011 | 2012

105

ADDING PHOTOVOLTAICS

Due to the unexpected additional energy use, it was determined that adding more PV panels would be the only way to achieve net zero energy in a reasonable amount of time. The project made two additions from the original 12.1 kW system. In September 2011, eight additional panels totaling 1.8 kW were installed. This addition occurred about six months into the one-year Challenge clock. However, this addition was not enough to overcome a colder, darker winter than the years of meteorological data the team used for its PV production estimate. In fact, the NREL typical year, which uses the last thirty years of meteorological data of solar insolation and was used to estimate the Bertschi School PV system needs, seems to exaggerate the solar resource available in the non-summer months. The chart below outlines the predicted data against the actual measured solar radiation

near the Bertschi site. Combined with the additional building heaters' use, the reduced solar energy hurt the PV production.

Following the initial addition, in June 2012 the school added 7 kW to the system for a total of 20.1 kW. This new full system capacity was better aligned with the actual energy use of the building. However, this system was larger than the required total building load, which allowed the team to catch its net zero goal at a faster rate. With the new system, the Bertschi School made up a deficit of 1200 kWh in six months while continuing to use a total of 32,884 kWh in building energy after the additional panels were installed. These panels now ensure that the building operates as net positive, always producing more energy than it uses and sending the surplus back to the grid.

	NREL TYPICAL YEAR	2011 ACTUAL	2011 DIFFERENCE FROM NREL TYPICAL	2012 ACTUAL	2012 DIFFERENCE FROM NREL TYPICAL
January	1.54	0.761	-0.779	0.812	-0.728
February	2.50	1.68	-0.82	1.49	-1.01
March	3.71	2.44	-1.27	2.48	-1.23
April	4.37	3.79	-0.58	4.44	0.07
May	5.31	4.53	-0.78	5.57	0.26
June	5.52	4.98	-0.54	4.53	-0.99
July	5.88	5.51	-0.37	5.79	-0.09
August	5.17	5.59	0.42	5.74	0.57
September	4.98	3.93	-1.05	4.91	-0.07
October	3.00	1.78	-1.22	2.04	-0.96
November	1.76	1.06	-0.70	0.94	-0.82
December	1.26	0.67	-0.59	0.538	-0.722

106

* All units in kWh/m2/day
** Data in blue was under Living Building Challenge clock (the time it took Bertschi to reach net zero)
***Actual data collected from University of Washington monitoring equipment located 1.3 miles from Bertschi site

PV system on the Church Building

ENVELOPE TEST

When extra energy is expended for building heating, a leaky envelope might be to blame. To help rule out this possibility, the team brought back Medgar Marceau to investigate the envelope's air-tightness using a blower door test. This test replaces one of the building's exterior doors with a panel that has a powerful fan in it with pressure gauges connected to a computer. Prior to the test, each of the exterior doors, windows and other openings is sealed. The fan in the door pulls air out of the building, lowering the pressure inside which allows any exterior air to rush into the building. "The first test indicated that the overall air leakage was equivalent to a hole just slightly more than 1 foot by 1 foot," according to Medgar.

Once the building was depressurized during the second test, team members moved throughout the spaces with smoke pencils to locate where any leaks might be. To supplement the smoke pencils, they also used a thermal imaging infrared camera to see where cold spots were in the walls. Medgar's tests found that the measured air leakage rate was 0.45 cubic feet per minute per square foot of envelope area (under a nominal air pressure difference of 75 Pascals.) This rate is slightly more than the current energy code maximum of 0.40 cfm/ sq ft. The team meticulously worked through the building, sealing any small cracks with foam tape and insulation and, as Medgar explains, "we were confident we were down around the 0.1 cfm/sq ft, which in our experience is a very tight building." These important tests helped the team make small but significant improvements to the envelope to improve the overall energy efficiency.

Blower door and infrared camera testing

107

"When we didn't qualify for energy the first year, it was a big ah ha moment. The fifth graders went to every class to tell them why and told the fourth graders that it was up to them [to meet net zero energy] for the next year."

BRIGITTE BERTSCHI
Head of Bertschi School

A LIVING BUILDING IS A LEARNING BUILDING... FOR ALL

In spite of tireless efforts, the Bertschi team did not achieve net zero energy at the end of our first twelve months of measured operation. Naturally, team members were disappointed, feeling that they had let the school and students down. But, not to be deterred, we got back to work and ended up learning a great deal during the additional months of effort to get to net zero.

"We took a leap of faith and dared to be wrong," says Tiffany Carey. "We talked to the kids about daring to be wrong and that if you fail it's okay; it's a learning opportunity." It was important to the design team that the building would be educational, not just when it was performing the way it was designed, but also in the times that it was not. After diligent tuning, sealing, measuring loads and reducing them, Bertschi achieved net zero energy in November 2012. This was the last remaining accomplishment on the road to Living Building Challenge Certification.

The Energy Petal: LEARNING TO CONSERVE AND GENERATE

THE HEALTH PETAL

Health Promotes Education

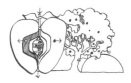

The Health Petal: **HEALTH PROMOTES EDUCATION**

SUMMARY OF THE LIVING BUILDING CHALLENGE VERSION 2.0 HEALTH PETAL

Petal Intent

The intent of the Health Petal is to focus on the major conditions that must be present to create robust, healthy spaces rather than to address all of the potential ways that an interior environment could be compromised. There is direct correlation between decreased comfort and increased environmental impacts, since solutions in the physical environment to improve well-being are often energy-intensive and wasteful.

Petal Imperatives

- Civilized Environment
- Healthy Air
- Biophilia

Living Building Science Classroom

IMPERATIVE:
CIVILIZED ENVIRONMENT

From the outset of the project, indoor air quality was just as significant a concern as the other sustainability features of the building. A classroom for students demands quality air not only for increased academic performance, but also to promote a healthy indoor environment for this sensitive group. Indoor air pollutants can cause discomfort and reduce school attendance and productivity. Moreover, they can "cause or contribute to short- and long-term health problems, including asthma, respiratory tract infection and disease, allergic reactions, headaches, nasal congestion, eye and skin irritations, coughing, sneezing, fatigue, dizziness and nausea."[37] And with an estimated "50 percent of the nation's schools having problems linked to poor indoor air quality," there is great potential for improvement with this basic necessity.[38]

The requirement to have operable windows in every regularly occupied space can be a difficult design feature to achieve but it has a variety of benefits for occupants. The Living Science Building relies on natural ventilation for cooling and fresh air. Natural ventilation is the use of a building's form, organization and openings in conjunction with naturally occurring phenomena such as the wind or warm air buoyancy to supply air to its occupants and to remove heat both from the occupants and the building.[39] There is also evidence that suggests that purely air-conditioned spaces may not be optimal for student health. In a recent study in a hot and humid climate, researchers found that students attending naturally ventilated childcare centers had lower levels of asthma symptoms and allergies than those in air-conditioned childcare centers.[40]

As an energy and health consideration, Bertschi's science building was designed to provide all of its cooling through natural ventilation. Each regularly occupied space has operable windows that students can open. To further facilitate the stack effect ventilation that draws air up and out of the room, the main skylight in the classroom space is also operable. When all of the windows and the skylight are open, the building has been successfully cooled during the warmer months.

37 United States Environmental Protection Agency. "Indoor Air Quality Tools for Schools: Actions to Improve Indoor Air Quality". Publication # 402-F-99-008. September 1999.
38 United States Environmental Protection Agency. "Indoor Air Quality Tools for Schools: Actions to Improve Indoor Air Quality". Publication # 402-F-99-008. September 1999.
39 Brown, G. Z. Natural Ventilation in Northwest Buildings. Eugene, OR.: University of Oregon, 2004. Print.
40 Zuraimi, M. S., Tham, K. W., Chew, F. T., & Ooi, P. L. (2007). The effect of ventilation strategies of child care centers on indoor air quality and respiratory health of children in Singapore. Indoor Air, 17(4), 317-327.

DAYLIGHTING

Of course, windows can affect the energy consumption of a building. Glazing, even when not operable, is much less thermally efficient than a solid wall that can be insulated. But while windows can be a disadvantage to energy use, they can also provide ample and wide-ranging benefits to occupants when designed properly.

The human health benefits can outweigh even the smallest trade-off in energy efficiency. In schools, there can be nothing more important in a building than a healthy environment for students. One study found that students without access to natural light showed a delay in seasonal cortisol production, a hormone that is positively associated with concentration abilities.[41] There are numerous studies that show a link between daylight or fresh air and student focus or higher test scores. In fact, having a view out of a window that includes vegetation, human activity or objects at a far distance help support better outcomes of student learning.[42] This is a perfect reason for the Bertschi students to look directly out onto their ethnobotanical garden right from their desks.

41 Kuller, R., & Lindsten, C. (1992). Health and behavior of children in classrooms with and without windows. *Journal of Environmental Psychology*,12, 305-317.
42 Heschong, Lisa. *Windows and Classrooms: A Study of Student Performance and the Indoor Environment*. Tech. Fair Oaks, CA: Heschong Mahone Group, 2003. Print.

114

Ecohouse with energy recovery ventilator, runnel and potable water cistern

IMPERATIVE:
HEALTHY AIR

Although natural ventilation is a good strategy for cooling and ventilating the Bertschi building, it does not work well for all seasons. To improve indoor air quality, building codes also require that a high rate of outside air be provided for schools.

There have been various studies that estimate the potential for a 5 to 10 percent increase in aspects of student performance with increased classroom ventilation rates. At Bertschi, increased indoor air quality was achieved by supplementing natural ventilation with the mechanical energy recovery ventilator system described earlier, providing 30 percent excess ventilation compared to the code required amount. This 425 cubic feet per minute rate translates to about two air changes per hour in the building. The Ecohouse is not a regularly occupied space, and does not have code required or ASHRAE required ventilation. However, to ensure some air change and help prevent the build-up of moisture in this space, the ERV relieves its air from the classroom into the Ecohouse, which then has a motorized damper (controlled to open when the ERV is operating) to allow that air to vent outside. To help the students monitor all of this air change, wall-mounted sensors with displays provide information on space temperature, humidity and CO_2 levels.

The building also uses a purely natural method to clean the air: the plants of the green wall. In addition to creating a self-sustaining water management system, these plants also provide students as much clean oxygen as three 14 foot tall trees and will clean over 34 pounds of dust and harmful toxins in the air per year.[43]

Indoor pollution sources that release gases or particles into the air are the primary cause of indoor air quality problems.[44] These particles can be greatly reduced by employing point-source reduction. Many of these harmful particles are brought into buildings on shoes. Permanent entryway systems can help to reduce these contaminates. These walk-off mats and grates placed at building entries help to remove the particles before they are brought into a space where they may become airborne. Bertschi utilizes both permanent systems and removable mats to reduce harmful particles.

The required air quality testing for a Living Building is extensive and rightly so. In addition to testing air quality prior to occupancy, it is required that the building be tested again once occupied and operating for at least twelve months. The tests completed for the Bertschi School measured formaldehyde, carbon monoxide, 53 volatile organic compounds (VOCs) and respirable suspended particulate matter small enough to enter human lungs. The importance of these tests cannot be overstated. By following strict construction procedures and using materials that were free of toxins, the Bertschi building passed all air quality tests.

115

43 "Bertschi School." *GSky Plant Systems Inc RSS.*
   N.p., n.d. Web. 05 Jan. 2014.

44 Indoor Air Quality: An Introduction to IAQ."
   EPA. Environmental Protection Agency,
   18 Nov. 2013. Web. 05 Jan. 2014.

IMPERATIVE:
BIOPHILIA

Biologist E.O Wilson coined the term Biophilia in 1984 and defines it as "the innate tendency to focus on life and lifelike processes." The Living Building Challenge describes it as the elements that nurture the innate human attraction to natural systems and processes. Biophilia has been categorized into six design elements and plays a significant role in the Bertschi Living Science Classroom. While the building boasts several of the design attributes from each of the six biophilic design elements, the Environmental Features element is most heavily represented.

ENVIRONMENTAL FEATURES

WATER collects as rain falls on the building roof, then flows through internal rain leaders to the runnel in the classroom floor on its way to cisterns, with overflow going to the rain garden. This design brings the hydrologic cycle right to the classroom allowing the students to watch the water fall from the sky and flow back to the earth.

AIR also plays a role in the building with every space having access to fresh air through natural ventilation. Opening windows allows the students to feel gentle breezes and hear the rustling of plants in the garden just outside.

PLANTS are a major element throughout the Bertschi building. In the Ecohouse, an entire wall of tropical plants is used to treat the greywater in the building. In addition to interior plants, the exterior ethnobotanical garden provides a source of food and native implements.

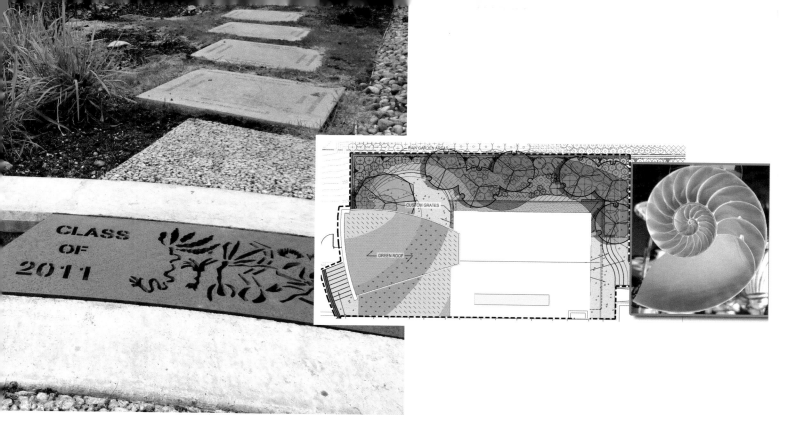

NATURAL SHAPES AND FORMS

BOTANICAL MOTIFS The science building took a unique approach to the botanical motifs element of Biomimicry. Rather than using traditional building elements to represent plants, the designers cast a variety of local leaves into the concrete slab of the Ecohouse. Students take rubbings of the detailed impressions left behind by these native species, which provide another reminder of nature within the space.

SHELLS AND SPIRALS The elegant and recognizable form of the nautilus was chosen to represent the shell and spiral element of biophilia on the project. This form was intended to be viewed from the fourth and fifth grade classrooms that overlook the science building. The shape is included in both the planting pattern of different mosses in the moss mat roof as well as the spiral shape of the exterior classroom and runnel in the garden.

NATURAL PATTERNS AND PROCESSES

INFORMATION RICHNESS The science building was designed to present a world of information richness and spark curiosity in the students who use it. Natural elements abound throughout the building, begging to be explored and touched by students. The rock-lined runnel with flowing rainwater, the green wall of tropical plants, natural materials, imprints of plants and castings of salmon and beetles, the variety of edible plants in the garden and even the unnatural digital elements of the meters that track the natural elements of sun and rain all provide many opportunities for learning about the natural and built environments.

Abundant natural light and connection to the outdoors is always present.

The runnel flows directly into the Ecohouse

118

LIGHT AND SPACE

NATURAL LIGHT is a major feature in the classroom. The building boasts 100 percent daylighting in all regularly occupied spaces with an average daylight factor of over 4 percent. This natural light not only saves energy but also has proven results of increasing academic performance and health in schools. A primary benefit to the daylighting that the building receives is that is it predominantly all north light. This orientation eliminates most glare as well as sun spots that could either distract students or create temperature fluctuations.

INSIDE-OUTSIDE SPACES The Ecohouse was designed to act as an inside-outside space to blur the line between nature and the built environment. Originally conceived by the school as a simple green house structure apart from the building, the Ecohouse developed into a space that celebrates nature, the scientific explorations in the curriculum and some of the building's processes. Directly linked with the instructional classroom space, the Ecohouse has a wall full of tropical plants and also provides heated grow cabinets for plant and soil studies. The large curtain wall provides excellent views of the ethnobotanical rain garden and the eight foot wide double doors open out to a porous paved surface to create an outdoor classroom.

PLACE-BASED RELATIONSHIPS

CULTURAL CONNECTION TO PLACE
For the Bertschi Science Building, the ethnobotanical garden was born out of a biophilic cultural connection to place. The native garden is connected to the geography and ecology of the region and to its history. Specific native plants were selected that were used by the native people of Seattle — the first inhabitants. This garden has also helped to cross curriculum, allowing the art department to take advantage of the garden.

SPIRIT OF PLACE While the spirit of place is a difficult design attribute to capture, the design team believes the Bertschi Science Building is a true example of this attribute. The building was designed to exude nature; to fill the space with natural light and air; to bring living plants and running water inside. It is a building that is of nature, built within nature and supports nature.

EVOLVED HUMAN-NATURE RELATIONSHIPS

EXPLORATION AND DISCOVERY/ CURIOSITY AND ENTICEMENT Perhaps one of the best ways the Bertschi building reveals itself is through biophilia with exploration and discovery apparent throughout the design. The idea that nature is the most intellectually stimulating environment that people encounter is one of the primary objectives of the building. As a science classroom, it encourages children to explore and interact. Much of the science curriculum is earth- and technology-based and the building helps students to be a part of their curriculum. With flowing water, growing plants and photovoltaic power at their fingertips, the students are immersed in science and can explore and discover what appeals to each of them.

CHANGE AND METAMORPHOSIS Because the building is rooted with natural systems and expresses natural elements even within its walls, change and metamorphosis is inherent. The students see the changing flows of water within the runnel. They watch the plants grow, adapt, function and sometimes die. They witness the edible plants adapt to the changing seasons and harvests. The moss species on the roof changes color, blooms and welcomes wind-blown seeds to sprout. The electrical needs are influenced by the changing weather and the classroom's uses. No matter where the students look, the natural elements of the Bertschi Science Building are always changing — just like the students themselves.

THE MATERIALS PETAL

In Search of Healthy Materials

Greenwall

The Materials Petal: IN SEARCH OF HEALTHY MATERIALS

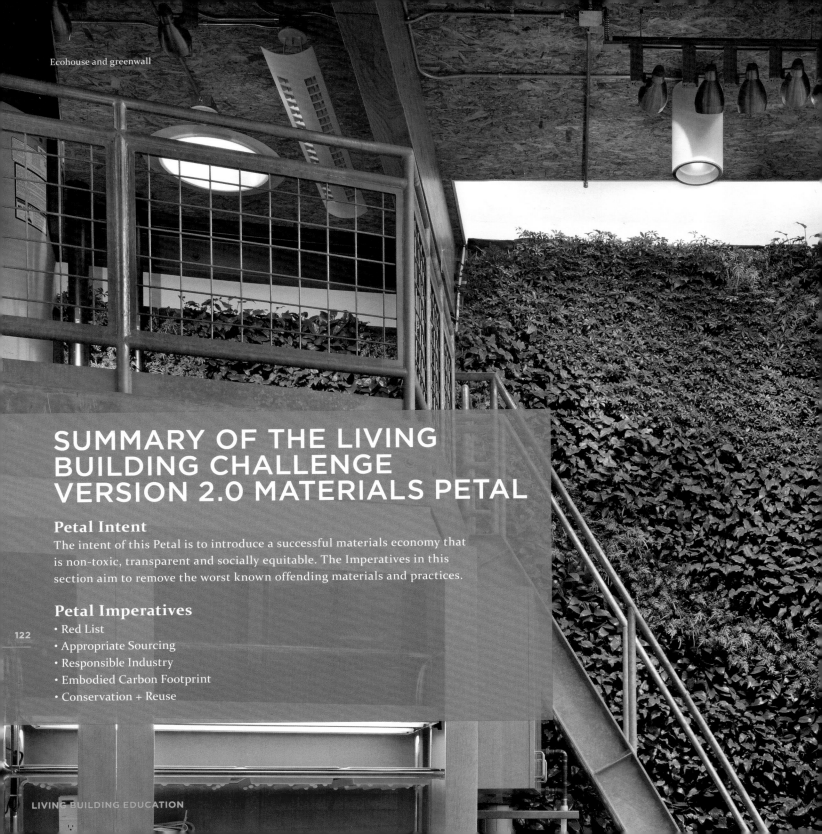

SUMMARY OF THE LIVING BUILDING CHALLENGE VERSION 2.0 MATERIALS PETAL

Petal Intent

The intent of this Petal is to introduce a successful materials economy that is non-toxic, transparent and socially equitable. The Imperatives in this section aim to remove the worst known offending materials and practices.

Petal Imperatives

- Red List
- Appropriate Sourcing
- Responsible Industry
- Embodied Carbon Footprint
- Conservation + Reuse

122

"It always seems impossible until it's done."

NELSON MANDELA

IN SEARCH OF HEALTHY MATERIALS

It has been said that great achievement has no roadmap. The Living Building Challenge is no exception. Sometimes, in order to push the boundaries of current thinking and practice, designers need to break away from convention. When Living Building design teams are asked what the most difficult part of the Living Building Challenge is, the Materials Petal stands alone.

"The materials were by far the most challenging aspect of the project, and they continue to be," says Steve Clem of Skanska. "The construction supply chain has developed into a confusing global web that values exotic materials with harmful chemicals made half a world away." When compared to some of the other Imperatives — Net Zero Energy, Net Zero Water or Urban Agriculture for example, there are engineered solutions readily available to achieve these goals. PV panels can be installed to meet energy needs, roofs can be used to collect rainwater and indigenous plants can be cultivated to grow food. However, the Imperatives of the Materials Petal rely on the willingness of the industry to achieve the requirements.

123

THE DESIGN PROCESS

There is often a disconnect between architectural practice and research. There is not enough time for research during typical projects and the time needed is much different than the time designers are accustomed to spending. The appetite that typical clients, budgets and design teams have for investigation is not to the level required for in-depth materials investigation. However, few design practitioners committed to using revolutionary materials exploration are trained as chemists. The knowledge and expertise required to understand the ramifications of various chemicals and toxins in the built environment is extensive.

Initially, the Bertschi design team did not know there was a need to change the process. Before the project began, the team understood that building materials have the potential to be harmful to the environment, thus the Materials Petal would be difficult. To help combat these issues, the team decided to limit the amount of finish materials. As Stacy says, "it supported our desire for the building to be an honest and transparent teaching tool."

One of the design team's greatest lessons came from the Materials selection process. Mistakenly, the team followed the typical process of designing to particular building products and materials and specifying products during the final phases of the design process. From there, a contractor would follow the specifications during construction and submit products to the architect for review that would meet the specifications. This is not the most effective process to follow for the Challenge. "Because this was the first time any of us were attempting the Challenge, we were naïve to the level of research necessary to really understand the chemical make-up and sourcing of a material. We relied on MSDS [Material Safety Data Sheets] and available sourcing information (usually published to LEED standards) to vet materials for our specifications," explains Stacy. Unfortunately and too often, the team learned that the MSDS sheets did not disclose all of the chemicals in a product and the LEED sourcing information

did not track the extraction locations. This data insufficiency led to the team being unprepared and Skanska having a greater burden during construction to find the needed product data. Skanska Project Manager Kris Beason says, "The contractor team quickly realized that industry standards had never undergone such scrutiny. Thousands of hours were expended to educate manufacturers on Living Building requirements, and the need to eliminate the substances on the materials Red List. Manufacturers were often hesitant to disclose details about the composition of products without first consulting their legal teams."

The Challenge demands far greater rigor during the early stages of design. Ideally, the contractor would work alongside the design team during the design stages to thoroughly vet materials prior to the completion of the contract documents.

When the design team began to request the ingredients of the products, it was a pioneering process taking materials transparency for an entire building to new levels. There were no third party transparency evaluation tools such as Healthy Product Declarations or ILFI's Declare label to help designers untrained in chemistry or materials science, so the burden of education and data extraction fell to the team alone.

124

"I think the most challenging part of the Red List was the inability to trust the data we were getting from suppliers."

STEVE CLEM
VP of Preconstruction, Skanska

IMPERATIVE:
RED LIST

Over the last few years, I have spoken to a lot of school groups, adults and hundreds of children regarding the Living Building Challenge. When I discuss the Materials Petal, I show the Red List of fourteen commonly used chemicals that cannot be used in a Living Building and ask if anyone recognizes any chemical listed. No matter how old they are, students recognize PVC (polyvinyl chloride or vinyl).

I ask them where they might have seen this material used and they easily associate it with piping. It is disheartening to think that one of our most toxic and commonly used building materials can be recognized by children. Should they not be able to easily recognize bamboo instead? Or cork? Or examples of biophilia?

According to the Healthy Building Network, "PVC is the worst plastic from an environmental health perspective posing unique and major hazards in its manufacture, product life and disposal. PVC has contributed a significant portion of the world's burden of persistent toxic pollutants and endocrine-disrupting chemicals including dioxin and phthalates — that are now universally present in the environment and the human population."[45]

Many of these toxic chemicals are known as persistent bioaccumulative toxins (PBTs). These chemicals can travel long distances through the atmosphere and water, eventually settling sometimes far from where they originally were manufactured. In addition to being persistent, PBTs bioaccumulate, which means they build up in living organisms through air, soil, water

45 "Healthy Building Network: PVC Facts." *Healthy Building Network:* PVC Facts. N.p., 2012. Web. 20 Jan. 2014.

THE PROJECT CANNOT CONTAIN ANY OF THE FOLLOWING RED LIST MATERIALS OR CHEMICALS:

- Alkylphenols
- Asbestos
- Cadmium
- Chlorinated Polyethylene and Chlorosulfonated Polyethlene
- Chlorobenzenes
- Chlorofluorocarbons (CFCs) and Hydrochlorofluorocarbons (HCFCs)
- Chloroprene (Neoprene)
- Chromium
- Chlorinated Polyvinyl Chloride (CPVC)
- Formaldehyde (added)
- Halogenated Flame Retardants (HFRs)
- Lead (added)
- Mercury
- Polychlorinated Biphenyls (PCBs)
- Perfluorinated Compounds (PFCs)
- Phthalates
- Polyvinyl Chloride (PVC)
- Polyvinylidene Chloride (PVDC)
- Short Chain Chlorinated Paraffins
- Wood treatments containing Creosote, Arsenic or Pentachlorophenol
- Volatile Organic Compounds (VOCs)

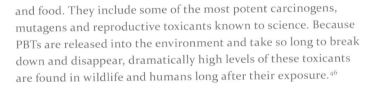

and food. They include some of the most potent carcinogens, mutagens and reproductive toxicants known to science. Because PBTs are released into the environment and take so long to break down and disappear, dramatically high levels of these toxicants are found in wildlife and humans long after their exposure.[46]

Flame retardant compounds containing other hazardous chemicls are also too pervasive in household furniture and building insulations. Some of these chemicals, like the Red Listed halogenated variety are bioaccumulative toxins that have shown to cause endocrine disruption, immunotoxicity, reproductive toxicity, cancer and adverse effects on fetal and child development and neurologic function.[47] Recent investigations have shown that the use of these toxic flame retardants has no impact on actually preventing fires in the products that

contain them and that their use has long been perpetuated by chemical industries distorting science for financial gain.[48]

The difficulty with Red List investigation is trying to find the ingredients in building products. But now this situation is improving because people are asking for transparency in their governments, financial systems, food labeling and, increasingly, in products. Although the obstacles for the Bertschi project team were numerous, there certainly were some successes through the difficulty of the Red List. The team identified useable skylights from a local company, Crystalite, in nearby Everett, Washington. Although a gasket in the skylight contained neoprene, a Red List material, Crystalite agreed to change their product and remove the neoprene from the skylight after the team familiarized the company with the Challenge.

126

46 *Toxic Chemicals in Building Material:s An Overview for Health Care Organizations.* Publication. Healthy Building Network, May 2008. Web.
47 "Health & Environment." *Green Science Policy.* N.p., 2013. Web.

48 Callahan, Patricia, and Sam Roe. "Playing With Fire." *Chicago Tribune* 6 May 2012: n. pag.Green Science Policy. Web.

APPROPRIATE SOURCING

Going well beyond any previous standard to consider sourcing, the Appropriate Sourcing Imperative is important because it considers where materials are both extracted and fabricated. Once the design team investigated Red List compliance for a material, it needed to then make sure each product could be found within the appropriate distance from the Bertschi site.

While many building products are made in Western Washington and along the Pacific coast, there are a surprising number of common products that are not made nearby at all. For example, hollow metal exterior doors could not be sourced within the appropriate distance. The closest locations for the two types needed were California and Iowa. The team also found a sourcing issue with its greywater treatment boxes. There are very few products on the market to meet these needs. The Aqua2 model that the team required comes from Taiwan, which is too far to meet Appropriate Sourcing requirements. The team's research to find alternative products led to only two that are regionally made. Flotender (manufactured in Woodinville, Washington) and Brac (manufactured in Montreal, Quebec). The Flotender unit is not recommended for indoor use required by the Bertschi project and the pump is larger than needed. The Brac system was also too large and uses Red Listed chlorine. Although the team did not use Flotender, the members worked with the company to educate them about the Red List concerns of PVC, which they subsequently removed from their product line. In

order to get exterior doors and greywater treatment appropriate for the building required the team to use an exception. In Challenge terms, this exception is known as "jumping a zone" to use a product located farther from the building site. Like the hopes of the Red List, Appropriate Sourcing seeks to improve the manufacturing industry by making healthy products available within appropriate distances from building projects.

Rather than jumping a zone, the Challenge really encourages creative and ecological ways to meet the Materials Petal whenever possible. When the design team was unable to find the required steel for the handrails and the ship's ladder in the Ecohouse within the project's Appropriate Sourcing radius, it used a method of procurement that every project should practice — the use of salvaged material. Alliance Steel in nearby Tacoma, Washington found salvaged material languishing in its yard that was able to be fabricated into these items. The use of this salvaged material eliminated the need for new steel and it also eliminated the possibility of the material being sent to a landfill.

127

WORKING WITH MANUFACTURERS

Once again, Bertschi's integrated design team makes the Living Building Challenge achievable. Without the help of the general contractor, Skanska, the team would not have been as successful with the Materials Petal.

Skanska created a form that was sent to each manufacturer. This form explained the detailed requirements of the Challenge's Red List and Appropriate Sourcing Imperatives and had space for the manufacturers to list all of the ingredients in their product and the location for both extraction and manufacturing. However, simply sending this form alone with the request for information would not be sufficient. Skanska had to put continuous pressure on manufacturers that only a billion dollar, multi-national company with 57,000 employees could do. When dealing with manufacturers just as large, it sometimes took the global influence of Skanska to pressure them into releasing their product components or sometimes just simply to respond. Skanska also had a great relationship with the local subcontractors and manufacturers. "The smaller manufacturers were a huge key to our success with the Living Building Challenge," explains Kris Beason. "Unlike some of the larger, Fortune 500 manufacturers," she says, "there was no hesitation from the smaller companies to fully disclose material information. These companies were also very open-minded to modifying materials as necessary to be Red List compliant."

CONSTRUCTION IS HALTED

During construction, concerns about the Red List and Appropriate Sourcing Imperatives become heightened. Without a completely defined specification to Red List standards, the team encountered its first and only construction delays.

During an on-site electrical inspection, a Seattle city inspector advised the design team that the aluminum conduit to be placed below grade did not meet code. The team was planning to install this particular conduit because, unlike standard metal conduit, it was not galvanized. Galvanization is a common process of zinc-coating metal to protect it from rust and corrosion, a process that often involves cadmium, which is a Red List item. Thus, the use of galvanized metal was not allowed by the Living Building Challenge. Other conduit types were not allowed by Seattle and they would have also been cost-prohibitive. After working with ILFI through the Dialogue, the design team was able to gain an exception to allow galvanization. This temporary exception applied unilaterally to all Challenge projects only if the galvanized metal could be protected from soil and water contamination. For Bertschi, that meant that any of the below-grade, required conduit had to be fully encased in concrete.

Not long after the team had overcome the conduit delay, a bigger issue was discovered during construction. While installing the below-grade domestic water piping (for which there were only two code-allowed products, one which contained PVC and

the other which did not have any Red List materials), the team encountered a sourcing problem. So many times when it was trying to gather Red List and Appropriate Sourcing data from manufacturers, there were long delays before the team received full responses. Sometimes, this meant that the team needed to push forward with construction when it did not have all of the data. This was the case with the domestic water piping. Here, the team had a product that met Red List requirements — one of only two code-allowed options that did so. But while installing it, the manufacturer had finally responded to the team's request made long before and confirmed that the product was made in Germany, well outside of the Appropriate Sourcing distance. Construction was forced to stop because this was a pipe to be installed below grade, and the contractors could not continue the next sequence of events that would ultimately cover this pipe and allow construction to continue. After an extensive search (with the help of the subcontractor) for a compliant product, a compliant pipe made in Minnesota was found. All this research took time and the construction delay resulted in a full month being added to the project finish date.

129

The groundbreaking ceremony

"The Materials Petal is the greatest challenge to project teams because the materials ecosystem requires a fundamentally different model from the one in current operation."

EDEN BRUKMAN
Co-author, Living Building Challenge

CAN WE REALLY DO THIS?

Even with a dedicated team, gathering the right information for the Materials Petal is extremely difficult. Often, the requests for product ingredients went unanswered. Sometimes, the team was told that the list of ingredients and chemicals were "proprietary," meaning that companies could hide behind claims of business interests to protect their intellectual property.

Even when responses were received from companies, they were not necessarily what team members wanted to hear. After trying to investigate products thought to meet Red List or Appropriate Sourcing from the little information that a manufacturer was voluntarily releasing, the team would be surprised by a hidden toxic ingredient that showed up on the Red List. This process repeated itself frequently. The team spent countless hours finding products or materials to meet the design intent only to discover they were not Red List compliant. It became emotionally taxing for everyone. There were times when team members could not find alternate products and it seemed as if the Materials Petal could not be met with current market limitations. The team faced giving up on the Materials Petal.

Stacy Smedley, Chris Hellstern & Joel Sisolak at the groundbreaking

JASON AND EDEN INSPIRE THE TEAM

The team had come to a crossroad. It was not the barrier of being prohibited to drink our collected rainwater or finding local wood; it was the unwilling manufacturing industry that was seemingly preventing us from meeting our Living Building goals. The team was discouraged and disappointed.

At this time the team reached out to Jason F. McLennan and Eden Brukman at the Institute, asking for a conference call to update them on its materials struggle and to get their advice. They told the team that, for the project to move forward and be successful, it needed to be comfortable using its best judgment determining when due diligence had been achieved and when a decision could be made without a cut-and-dried answer from ILFI Dialogue. The goal of the Challenge, they said, is not to interfere with a building's long-term performance. The choices made to meet Living Building standards must

only strengthen the building and support its functions for the owner. The team's first obligation was to create a proper school building and satisfy the goals of the project; the Living Building Challenge was secondary.

The team also presented its idea of due diligence to them, proposing that it could decide upon a guideline of research to follow when searching for a compliant product. This conference call served to reinvigorate the team and gave team members inspirition that they could, in fact, achieve the Material Petal.

"The Bertschi project team worked relentlessly to source building materials that complied with Imperatives 11 and 14."

EDEN BRUKMAN
Co-author,
Living Building Challenge

131

EDEN BRUKMAN
Co-author, Living Building Challenge

DUE DILIGENCE — A PROCESS IS CREATED

Creating a process of due diligence for materials research was essential for the design team to be successful. The Bertschi School project began Materials Petal information gathering and documentation before any procedural system was developed by the ILFI. Because of this timing, the Bertschi team developed its own method of documentation that worked with the contractor's procedures.

Information from the Living Building Challenge Dialogue and conversations with ILFI's Eden Brukman during the project's construction were used to organize our system. Challenge information pertaining to Red List and Appropriate Sourcing was collected on every single product used in the Bertschi Living Building. This information was compiled in a spreadsheet and used during design and construction to track Challenge compliance on all submittals. The team determined that it would look for three alternate products when searching for Red List and Appropriate Sourcing compliance. It also determined that meeting Red List compliance was the priority in materials selection and that sourcing would be a secondary concern. The members felt that it was more important to support healthy materials and work for the elimination of toxins in our products. As these healthy materials continue to develop in popularity, more widespread sourcing of these materials would follow the increased consumer demand for non-toxic products.

In cases where an MSDS sheet showed that a product met Challenge Materials Red List and Appropriate Sourcing Imperatives, the team required a signed letter from the manufacturer stating that the product meets the Red List

and is sourced within the appropriate zone. At the same time, the designated project team member whose discipline was associated with the product would find three alternate products from the next zone and document readily available published information regarding materials in the products. If a letter was not received and the three alternate zone-jumped products offered the same amount of information as the specified product, the specified product would be used.

Considering all of the team's attempts to reach out and educate manufacturers to the Living Building Challenge, then waiting for responses that often never came, sifting through distracting and obfuscating data, and searching for local and compliant products, it spent an average of eight hours of research for every product and material in the Bertschi Science Wing. There are more than 275 unique products in the building. Of all these products, only 15 of them had to be granted an exception for Living Building Challenge Imperative compliance due to current market limitations. This unusual and unsustainable effort of research occupied three full-time Skanska employees in addition to Stacy and me to complete.

IMPERATIVE:
RESPONSIBLE INDUSTRY

Similar to the Habitat Exchange and Embodied Carbon Footprint Imperatives, Responsible Industry recognizes the reality of the global economy. Responsible Industry aims to advocate for third-party certified standards for resource extraction and fair labor practices in the materials industries of stone, rock, metal and timber. This effort aims to support the triple bottom line or three legs of the sustainability stool.

At this point in the Responsible Industry's development, there is a limit to the sustainable advancements of these materials industries. Therefore, the Challenge is advocating for a change in practice, much like the goals of the Red List. For industries that do not yet have standards in place, project teams are required to send one letter to the corresponding national trade association for each industry sector and ASTM International.

The second and more influential portion of Responsible Industry to Bertschi's Living Building comes through the requirement to

provide only FSC-certified wood throughout the entire project. The Forest Stewardship Council (FSC) is a global, not-for-profit organization dedicated to the promotion of responsible forest management worldwide. Essentially, the organization "works to improve forest management worldwide, and through certification creates an incentive for forest owners and managers to follow best social and environmental practices. This incentive brings direct benefits to the forest, such as protecting biodiversity, indigenous peoples' rights, workers' rights, and

133

FSC wood

134

areas of significant environmental or cultural importance."[49] There simply is no substitute in forest certification standards for the level of environmental and social protection that FSC provides.

This Imperative yielded some of the most surprising lessons for the project. For a building located in the heavily forested Northwest — the Evergreen State — the team found it extremely difficult to find FSC lumber to meet its needs. In fact, one of the first places team members found that could provide the FSC lumber needed for the exterior cedar siding was in Sweden. Team members discovered that sourcing FSC lumber can be problematic even though the demand for all types of FSC wood is and has been great. But, according to suppliers, the ability to obtain a consistent supply can often be an issue. Numerous limitations exist depending upon the type of lumber required. A particular roadblock occurred for the Bertschi team when it was trying to procure standard 4'x8' sheets of OSB (oriented strand board) for roof panels. At the time when this wood was needed, there was only one factory in the United States that milled it — but it had recently closed. After more research, the team found a Canadian supplier, the only company in North America that could supply this wood by the required deadline. Following the team's request, both the supplier and the SIP fabricator went through the process of obtaining full FSC chain of custody certification and can now provide these products to the marketplace. When the search for exterior wood trim began, the team had to reduce the quality of wood by one grade in order to meet the FSC requirements. Each of these lengthy searches and investigations for wood required the help of some of the top staff at the FSC organization. As a result of the Bertschi project, new connections have been made among the contractor, subcontractors and suppliers. The project's strict requirements pushed team members to look outside of the typical supply chains and form new relationships. Once again, one of the underlying themes of The Challenge has become apparent — people. To improve future projects, the team learned that the availability of FSC wood in a particular region should be analyzed during the design phase, something that is not typical.

Not every project can or should have to do this amount of research and procurement investigation. Especially in the forested Northwest, procuring FSC-certified wood should not be this difficult and this is one of the many improvements to the industry that the Challenge endeavors to make.

49 "Forest Stewardship Council®International Center." *FSC Forest Stewardship Council* ® · *Importance of Forest Stewardship*. N.p., n.d. Web. 18 Jan. 2014.

Bertschi Center's
PV and green roof

IMPERATIVE:
EMBODIED CARBON FOOTPRINT

Similar to the Habitat Exchange Imperative, the Embodied Carbon Footprint recognizes that buildings must still be built. This Imperative offsets the total footprint of embodied carbon from its construction and projected replacement parts through a one-time offset.

With the help of a carbon offset organization, the team calculated that the Bertschi project would need to account for twenty-nine tons of carbon emissions. According to the offset organization, preventing these greenhouse gases is the environmental equivalent of removing six average cars from U.S. roadways for one year. Although this may be a relatively small offset, every environmentally positive step made is important. Bertschi is now carbon neutral in both its operations and construction.

Workers meticulously hand-sorted all construction waste

"These stringent requirements are important to advancing C&D diversion rates, in whole, by bringing the responsibility of construction waste management back to the construction site, not just the sorting facilities themselves. With the focus on specific loads from the project being analyzed, the Challenge requirements are driving projects to design the building, strategize for waste minimization and execute the plan daily to meet diversion goals."

CHRIS EDLIN
Sustainability Advisor,
O'Brien & Company

IMPERATIVE:
CONSERVATION + REUSE

Conservation and Reuse has two important components. During construction, project teams must divert a specified percentage of material categories from landfills.

Project sustainability consultant Chris Edlin explains it this way: "In general, other environmental building rating systems are required to only track the monthly diversion rate of the facility where the project waste is taken. This system does not hold a project responsible for anything except delivery of their waste to the diversion facility. The Living Building Challenge's Conservation + Reuse Imperative requires that you track all project waste through load-specific analysis and divert various building materials to very high percentages, depending on the material. This process engages the project in determining waste streams, identifying viable markets for reclaimed materials, and creates a strategy of minimizing waste from the site."

But this is not just a straightforward diversion. Materials cannot be sent to any source that may repurpose the waste through the use of combustion. This requirement is where the Bertschi project first ran into difficulty. Seattle has a great history of being able to recycle at some of the highest rates in the country, often surpassing LEED standards. And while that may be a great improvement for so many jurisdictions, it is not sufficient for the Challenge. "As this project was the first of its kind in the Seattle area," reminds Chris Edlin, "the C&D [Construction and Demolition] facilities were not accustomed to the requirements of tracking waste to the degree required by the

CONSTRUCTION WASTE MATERIAL	TOTAL WASTE GENERATED (LBS)	AMOUNT DIVERTED FROM LANDFILL (LBS)	% DIVERTED
Metals	2,224	2,224	100
Paper/Cardboard	1,385	1,385	100
Soil/Biomass	180	180	100
Rigid Foam, Carpet, Insulation	300	300	93.3
All Other Combined Weighted Average	4,2112	37,562	89.2

Living Building Challenge. This held true on-site too, as the trades had to understand their role in separating the waste to ensure success in the diversion goals of the project."

Additionally, some of the waste that is diverted in the Seattle area is sent upstate to agricultural areas to be used as livestock fuel or incinerated. Local companies had to make special provisions to alter their typical process. But most significantly, because of the materials category requirements, all of the Bertschi construction waste had to be sorted by hand. This

hand-sorting effort was a considerable achievement. Frequently, Skanska, their subcontractors and the waste diversion company workers could be seen meticulously separating each piece of construction waste into its appropriate piles. All 46,200 pounds of construction waste, well under average for this building type, was sorted by hand at the Recovery 1 facility, which garnered a 100 percent diversion rate for most categories. Even at one of the largest construction waste facilities in Puget Sound, the Bertschi waste was given its own segregated location at the facility to help meet the Living Building Challenge requirements.

DESIGN PHASE

Designing a building pro bono and relying solely on community fundraising to meet construction costs was a great challenge. It was imperative that the team considered every design solution in a fiscally and environmentally responsible manner.

The requirement for natural, non-toxic and appropriately sourced materials also helped to support life-cycle considerations. Embodied energy of materials, as well as the overall building, were taken into consideration and then ultimately offset. The team's materials strategy was to omit finishes that were not necessary, exposing structural, mechanical, and electrical systems for educational and maintenance purposes.

Interior finishes, such as a wood ceiling and floor coverings, were eliminated to save unnecessary materials. For example, the team determined there was no need to cover the exposed

wood structure of the SIP roof panels with more wood simply for aesthetic purposes. Durable materials were used for structural components, including concrete slab, glu-lam structural columns and beams, and a SIP roofing system topped by a standing seam metal roof. Critical components that will see the most technological evolution in the market are also designed for easy adaptability. For example, the PV system, green wall, composting toilet, potable water treatment, greywater treatment and mechanical system are not permanently fixed to the building and all allow for disassembly and easy expansion or exchange of a newer system.

REUSE

Whenever possible, materials were reused or reclaimed for use on the Bertschi project.

RUNNEL PEBBLES

The pebbles that line the runnel, both interior and exterior, were reclaimed from a retail store once located in downtown Seattle. Before construction began on the Bertschi project, several of the design team members and contractors reclaimed the pebbles from the vacant store prior to its demolition. The pebbles were stored and cleaned before being hand-laid in the classroom.

CASEWORK

All casework used in the Bertschi project is composed of reclaimed fir salvaged from another job that the general contractor had previously worked on. That job was canceled and the material was slated for the landfill. Instead, it was rerouted to Bertschi's wood craftsmen, reassembled and refinished into the casework now used in the building.

MEZZANINE RAILING

The mezzanine railing and fencing material in the Ecohouse was reclaimed from various Seattle projects. The specified steel could not be located at the proper Challenge-compliant Appropriate Sourcing distance, so the local steel manufacturer salvaged components from scrap and fabricated them into the final designs now installed in the school.

RESTROOM TILE

The team worked with a local tile company to locate locally sourced tiling but had great difficulty achieving this objective. Most tile was found to be made in Europe or Asia or contain Red List items used for coloring. Instead, members of the design team visited the tile company's warehouse and combed through their waste piles. Several designs of tile were selected that were slated for the landfill and reused to completely tile the restroom in the Science Wing. This undertaking eliminated the need to create or purchase any new tile for this specific project and also diverted useable products from the landfill.

SITE GATE

During demolition of the existing site fence that surrounded the play court, some material was salvaged for later use. This material included wood fencing, steel posts and door hardware and closers. These items were repurposed and fashioned into the main gate that enters the Living Building site. The team went to great effort to salvage this material and repurpose it into what is now the public face for visitors who enter the site.

139

Bertschi students recycle and compost, tracking their own waste reductions each year

140

OPERATION PHASE

The school employs a rigid recycling and composting program created by the student body. Students learn to reduce, reuse, recycle and compost waste while learning about some of the larger global issues of waste streams.

Throughout the year students monitor consumption and waste. Students regularly weigh trash, analyzing the items thrown away. They graph their results and then make recommendations to the whole school about how to use fewer resources and how to properly sort waste for recycling and composting. For nearly twenty years, the school has been practicing a strict waste management program that includes education. The student-led program works to track and reduce waste and compost each year. All buildings on campus are equipped with appropriate recycling and compost containers and the students teach each other how to properly use them.

END OF LIFE PHASE

The Bertschi School Living Building has been designed with careful consideration given to the majority of the buildings' architectural and mechanical features to allow for easy upgrade or deconstruction and reuse if necessary.

The exterior cladding is a cedar siding rain screen system that can be carefully removed for reuse or replaced if necessary without harming the remaining envelope of the building. With an open floor plan, the school has the ability to make any room changes needed to accommodate programs. No demolition of interior walls would likely be required. If deconstruction or adaption became serious enough, the wood structure of the building could be disassembled. All of the glu-lam beams and columns are bolted together to form the structural system. These could be removed and the structural materials could be reused, allowing the building to be reconfigured.

In addition to deconstruction and reuse of the building's structure and envelope, the MEP systems can also be updated. Each system from ventilation to water treatment is left exposed for educational purposes which also offers the benefit of easy removal. The PV system

can be easily updated when more advanced models have been developed. The mounting systems can remain in place as new panels are installed. The majority of the water systems could also be easily removed for upgrade or deconstruction. The greywater units are simple boxes, as are the composting toilets. These can be easily removed without disturbing the rest of the building. The energy recovery ventilator is completely exposed in the Ecohouse and could be demounted and removed for update or reuse in another building without disturbing the rest of the project. The majority of piping and conduit has been left exposed and could be easily removed. The green wall is composed of individual planter boxes that can be lifted off the wall mounting racks. This design allows the plants to be replaced or relocated if the entire wall is deconstructed. The radiant floor system is controlled by a simple water tank-style heat pump that can be easily removed for upgrade or reuse elsewhere.

141

THE EQUITY PETAL

A Living Building is Equitable

143

SUMMARY OF THE LIVING BUILDING CHALLENGE VERSION 2.0 EQUITY PETAL

Petal Intent

The intent of the Equity Petal is to correlate the impacts of design and development to its ability to foster a true sense of community. A society that embraces all sectors of humanity and allows the dignity of equal access is a civilization in the best position to make decisions that protect and restore the natural environment.

Petal Imperatives

• Human Scale + Humane Places
• Democracy + Social Justice
• Rights to Nature

144

A LIVING BUILDING IS EQUITABLE

Equity sets the Living Building Challenge apart from all other rating systems and the typical considerations given to many of today's buildings. Conserving water and energy are important considerations for our buildings and the environment, but there is a missing element with this narrow perspective. Buildings are built for people. For a building to be truly sustainable, it must successfully incorporate considerations of the environment, economy and society. A Living Building is equitable for people and planet.

IMPERATIVE:
HUMAN SCALE + HUMANE PLACES

When asked what his favorite parts of the Living Building Challenge are, Stan Richardson said that he is, "glad that the Challenge addresses equity and human scale." From the outset, the Bertschi Living Building project team sought to create a building that was appropriately scaled for its user group — elementary students.

The design team not only kept these young stakeholders in mind, but also engaged the children in the design process, which generated a number of ideas that were incorporated into the project. In designing a space for young students, it was crucial that it be comfortable and not create distraction. The classroom was designed to provide a lecture space that is more appropriately sized for sitting while the tall Ecohouse space was scaled for standing experiments and to house the green wall that grows towards the sky. The project site is small and traditionally might have elicited a design that was lot line to lot line in order to maximize the space. But contrary to that practice, care was taken to ensure that the space was right-sized for the programmed use. This

approach saved materials and energy, while allowing for some natural landscape and low-impact development features.

Throughout the building, attention is given to child-scaled features. Windows are set low to allow views to the exterior and through to the Ecohouse while allowing for manual operation by students for ventilation. Scale considerations are taken beyond standard building features to other classroom items as well. Art pieces are located at student level, in some cases right on the floor, to promote interaction with various pieces. Overall, the science building is appropriately scaled for the entire Bertschi campus, which consists mostly of converted single-family homes. The Living Building fits well within this context and also matches the overall scale of the surrounding residential neighborhood.

IMPERATIVE:
DEMOCRACY + SOCIAL JUSTICE

Because of the nature of the building type, the Democracy + Social Justice Imperative presents some exciting opportunities.

As an urban school, Bertschi prioritizes security. The campus must be securely fenced for everyone's safety both inside and out. However, this security aspect does not mean that the school must present an inhospitable face to the neighborhood. The Science Wing, for example, is surrounded by a grated fence that allows for a transparent but secure connection between the school and its neighborhood. Urban agriculture of grapes and kiwi wind their way up the fence, providing a natural barrier that changes with the seasons. Although Bertschi School is closed to the general public, the school

draws its circle wide to welcome the community with various scheduled events, summer sustainability seminars and building tours. Graciously, Bertschi staff take time to open doors to anyone who wants to tour the building and campus, dedicating staff time to inspiring and educating the general public about building sustainability initiatives. The Living Building welcomes all, ensuring access for disabled persons to all features of the building. Buildings that are truly sustainable must encourage and promote a sense of community.

Collecting grapes along
the open site fence

IMPERATIVE:
RIGHTS TO NATURE

The idea behind the Rights to Nature Imperative is that all people should be allowed access to natural environments. The built environment should not inhibit the planet's ecosystems.

Shaded entirely by the historic church standing next to Bertschi School, the Living Building does not take away from adjacent sites but rather offers a good example of solar access rights. Because the church building infringes on the science wing's Rights to Nature, the net zero energy PV system was mounted on the neighboring building's south-facing roof in order to access sunlight.

The Living Building team was also careful not to allow the project site to restrict access to the natural water systems. In fact, the Bertschi site helps to manage more stormwater than the previous paved play court by handling some of the runoff from other parts of the campus. The campus water is actually directed through the Living Building and to its rain garden and allowed to naturally infiltrate back into the water table, helping to restore the pre-development conditions of the Cascade forest. Restoring Rights to Nature extends to living things at Bertschi as well. The rejuvenation of the site has brought about a return of many bird species, insects and even bees. A variety of grass and small plant seeds, dispersed by the wind, have landed on the moss mat roofs where they now thrive. Throughout the site, Bertschi's students and the community have ready access to nature. Their new building and site both protects and promotes nature for education and enjoyment of future generations.

147

THE BEAUTY PETAL

Beauty in Harmony

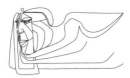

The Beauty Petal: **BEAUTY IN HARMONY**

SUMMARY OF THE LIVING BUILDING CHALLENGE VERSION 2.0 BEAUTY PETAL

Petal Intent

The intent of the Beauty Petal is to recognize the need for beauty as a precursor to caring enough to preserve, conserve and serve the greater good. As a society we are often surrounded by ugly and inhumane physical environments. If we do not care for our homes, streets, offices and neighborhoods then why should we extend care outward to our farms, forests and fields? When we accept billboards, parking lots, freeways and strip malls as being aesthetically acceptable, in the same breath we accept clear-cuts, factory farms and strip mines.

Petal Imperatives

• Beauty + Spirit
• Inspiration + Education

"What attracted me to the Living Building Challenge was the Beauty Petal and the calmness from a learning environment standpoint. That quality alone was really important."

BRIGITTE BERTSCHI
Head of Bertschi School

IMPERATIVE
BEAUTY + SPIRIT

At first glance, the Beauty Petal may not be what it seems. Often met with skepticism because it introduces subjectivity into a standard that otherwise focuses on measurable factors, this Petal is not about determining what may be classified as beautiful. Spirit, inspiration and educational outreach help to make a project align with this Imperative. Of course, beauty can be a controversial quality, especially when it might be judged in the context of the Living Building Challenge. But when designers infuse aspects of beauty into their designs, they are attempting to build meaning and working to make them last; the true measure of sustainability. The beauty of the Bertschi Science Wing stems from all the Imperatives of the Living Building Challenge working together in harmony. Just like the flower that represents the Challenge, beauty can be found when petals open to receive the sun's energy and stems grow taller with the renewing rain. When all of nature's systems join together and function as one, beauty is inherently the result.

151

Students Raise Salmon in Science Wing for Release

THE SPIRIT OF PRESERVATION AND EDUCATION

The Bertschi School Living Science Building has an honorable and necessary purpose. It exists for primary school education and aspires to teach not only science, but environmental stewardship as well. With a great foundation for this work as a whole, the Bertschi campus embodies a spirit of place.

Through renovation of historic homes, the overall campus is a celebration of culture and place by honoring the buildings that existed on its site before the school was there. The Living Building goes beyond that to honor the natural ecosystems of the Cascade forest that thrived long before humans arrived. The campus offers its students the opportunity to learn and play in buildings that range from early 1900s Craftsman homes and a mid-century church to the most innovative and sustainable buildings that are now possible — the latest of which the school's own students helped conceptualize.

For the students of Bertschi School, the beauty of their Living Science Building was born from their dreams. When the design team began our project, we started with the students. We asked them what a Living Building could and should be to showcase science. What would they dream about seeing in their classroom? How would they wish to see nature expressed? The students were inspiring and shifted the focus of what we, as designers, thought was possible. They asked for ideas that developed into some of the greatest design features of the building that not only perform functions and met LBC Imperatives but also exemplify and teach the beauty of nature.

Potable water cistern

Salmon casting along the runnel

NATURE AND REPRESENTATIONS OF NATURE

**Students learn that plants are not only beautiful to look at,
but that their beauty also comes from their function.**

These natural features represented in their classroom show the interconnectedness of the natural world. Our choices of how we use water have impacts on nature and the students can reach out and touch these affected living things from their desks. Just outside the classroom the students are surrounded by an ethnobotanical garden. Here, the changing patterns of nature are on full display as the students grow a variety of vegetables, fruits and indigenous plants.

Nestled quietly throughout the building and its garden's natural elements are artists' representations of nature. Throughout the Bertschi School's campus is a variety of artwork from local artists Judith and Daniel Caldwell, who have created some of the most well-known sculptures in Seattle. The Bertschi students study salmon during their science program, raising them from eggs until they can be released in local streams. To highlight this curriculum for a species that means so much to the Pacific Northwest, the design team asked the Caldwells to create bronze castings of all five salmon species. Each salmon is located in the classroom floor, following the curves of the runnel. The Red List-friendly lead-free bronze chosen for the sculptures was specified just as meticulously as each salmon was set into the concrete floor.

With the salmon swimming by the students' desks along the floor of the main classroom, we wanted some additional art pieces for the Ecohouse. For this installation, the Caldwells were asked to choose the subject. Coleoptera, the insect order commonly called beetles, was the obvious choice according to Judith. "With more species than any other order — about 400,000 — and a mind-boggling array of body types," Judith says, "it may have taken longer to pick out the ones we wanted to use than to make them.

153

Local plant leaves imprinted in the Ecohouse floor

154

We selected from among those hundreds of thousands of beetles the ones that were the most interesting morphologically to us, and attempted to express, within a small number of images, the incredible variety of beetles." Fifteen of these species crawl up the Ecohouse along the green wall. Quite coincidentally, Bertschi students study beetles, including a few of the exact species that are captured in bronze in their classroom.

To improve the industrial look of the manhole covers of the potable water cistern and water control valves in the classroom floors, the design team once again called on Judith and Daniel to create some inspirational images. The potable water cistern cover has a cast design of the water cycle to depict the Net Zero Water Petal processes that occur in the building. In the classroom, Judith says that, "the illustration of the human eye was favored because sight is both a literal and metaphorical pathway to knowledge." Also in the floor of the Ecohouse,

Stacy and I had one of the most enjoyable moments during the construction process as we precariously balanced over wet concrete to place indigenous leaves delicately in the floor. These impressions of a variety of species allow students to take rubbings of each leaf pattern.

It is not only professional artists who created inspirational pieces for the building. Bertschi students created art for the metal grate that covers the exterior runnel in the garden. Student-created kelp and sea anemone shapes are cut into curving metal plates. For this work of art, Bertschi fifth graders learned about the sea otter and how it is a keystone species for its ecosystem. From this study they each contributed a drawing for the permanent art project. As Stan Richardson points out, the beauty of children's representational art is that it "often allows adults to see familiar things through a fresh lens." Throughout the building, students are immersed in the beauty of art that pays tribute to nature.

THE STUDENTS DECIDE WHAT IS BEAUTIFUL

As designers of this innovative building, it may be a bit biased for design team members to declare Bertschi School's building beautiful. But the students feel this way as well. Anonymous surveys from the students reveal that the true spirit of place is apparent to the young students who experience it from this building every day. The most beautiful aspects of the building are the lessons and perspectives it instills in students. One student summed up the Imperative's success by saying simply: "We are living what we are learning."

As designers, Stacey and I, along with the other design team members, believe the Bertschi Living Building encompasses Beauty and Spirit in its story of creation, its built form and in the lessons it is able to teach students. Individually and collectively, we see the beauty embodied in the young students who can describe to their classmates the function of the composting toilet and the reason they use energy from the sun. We see the spirit of the Challenge and its environmental stewardship principles permeate the students' family lives as they implore their parents to turn off running water and unneeded lights at home and to compost their food scraps. The idea of this project evolved from the need to inspire and educate our future generations about buildings that contribute to a restorative future. We all hope that the Beauty and Spirit lessons of the Living Building Challenge will live on in the future generations; that is the true legacy of the project.

In many ways, Beauty and Spirit became personal to the Bertschi design team, the school's faculty and the students. We all have our own stories about the ways in which the Living Building Challenge framework and the building we designed, built and learn in has touched our lives and many of us will remember this experience forever.

Students collect garden berries for food and paint

"Evidence of the building's fulfillment of the Beauty Imperative abounds. In so many instances, the opportunity to delight users, enrich people's lives, and elevate spirits has been pursued. The result is that the Living Building is a great source of pride to the school, and it fans the community's awareness and commitment to conservation and sustainability."

BERTSCHI SCHOOL

STUDENT SURVEY QUOTES

"It helps me learn how to be kind to the earth."

"Our classroom has made me more aware of buildings that aren't living."

"It really lets us connect with the environment. It also plays a large role in teaching us how to take care of the environment. I now compost at my house."

"I love how it is so earthy. The building seems like it was constructed straight from nature."

155

Students help plant their garden

156

IMPERATIVE:
INSPIRATION + EDUCATION

Like the Imperatives of the Water Petal, the Beauty Petal's Inspiration and Education Imperative is one of my favorite parts of the Living Building Challenge.

From my time in Alaska teaching people about the Last Frontier's unsurpassed natural beauty to my thesis work in a sustainable elementary school, to my work on this project, education has been an important thread. Indeed, the Education Imperative of the Challenge is one of its most critical components, especially at this stage in the effort to transform the impact buildings have on the environment.

Before a single Living Building had been certified or Stacy and I had even realized the perfect opportunity presented by the Bertschi School, we wanted to create a Living Building that would be a teaching tool. We wanted to show that this type of building would be possible. We knew that it would be an education for ourselves and other team members and that it could be for others as well.

EXPOSED FEATURES

To accomplish this education objective, the design team aimed to have as many Imperatives and building features exposed to students as possible.

Of course there is the simplicity to exposing the processes with the river of collected rainwater flowing through the class and the solar panels on the roof. But upon closer inspection, once the students learn what is happening around them, they can discover the nuances of the plants in their classroom treating all the water they use. They watch the stormwater slowly infiltrate into their rain garden after watering their fruits and vegetables. Educational signage for nearly every Imperative is spread throughout the building and pipe labels show what water flows where. Meters are everywhere in the classrooms. The largest and most prominent is a black box in the class showing the students real-time energy use. Not only does this show them what is happening with energy, but also it helps the students understand their choices. As they turn on a light, they see the energy meter tick up. As they unplug a piece of equipment, they see the meter go down. "I like that it is all visible in the space and that the students are not only aware of its presence, but can identify the components and their function," says Nathan Miller. "It is great to connect the building users to all of the behind-the-scene systems and processes that are required to provide a modern standard of living." Students are gaining an understanding that what they do in buildings has consequences on their environment. Meters for water show how much rain has been collected in the potable water and irrigation cisterns and how much greywater is sent to the green wall. With supervision and through specific curriculum, the students perform experiments with the water in the cisterns. The impact of interacting with nature can set the course of these students' lives. In their Living Building, they have opportunities to work with plants, soil, water, energy and the endless lessons that they inspire.

The school has also done a remarkable job of trying to bring their Living Building to those who cannot visit it in person. With a comprehensive website, each feature is thoroughly explained, allowing people to virtually tour the project.

Infrared cameras used to locate any envelope heat loss

"I was inspired by the tenacity of the project team, and their willingness to learn — and teach. One of the project team's particular strengths was its ability to convene the local building industry and create a community united by a common mission."

EDEN BRUKMAN
Co-author, Living Building Challenge

"*I have been truly inspired by those who committed to making this project a reality. We all have so much to learn from the classroom, but I'm really looking forward to learning from the bright minds who come out of it.*"

COLLEEN MITCHELL
Civil Engineer,
2020 Engineering

Landsacape architect Zack Thomas of GGLO teaches Bertschi students how to plant their ethnobotanical garden

158

TEACHING STUDENTS ALONG THE WAY

One of the most rewarding parts of the project has been the journey with Bertschi's students, the community and our design team. Asking the students for their wish list was just the beginning of their involvement in the project.

Stacy and I were fortunate enough to attend classes and all-school meetings with the students of Bertschi, explaining the unique building they would soon have. We could see these visits having an impact as the children very quickly understood why they needed a building that could treat all of its water and use only energy from the sun. Some of them began to understand how to read our architectural drawings. I can recall one occasion when students were looking over the drawings we had on the table. One child was pointing to the plan to show his classmate where the "ethnobotanical garden was going." Another student corrected her classmate saying, "No, the composting toilet will be over here." Stacy and I were beaming with pride standing over their shoulders as they were talking about their new building. It was clear that they understood the extraordinary building they

were helping create. But perhaps most striking was that it seemed normal to them. To these young children, composting their blackwater, growing their food and building with healthy materials was just how things are done.

Of course, along the way, the students also taught us. From the very beginning design team members learned how to think like children and open their minds to untapped possibilities. The students pushed the design team to create legitimate function through their wish list items. They helped the team find ways to truly bring nature indoors and put natural processes at their fingertips. The students made the entire project a joy and never failed to inspire each of us. Nearly every day, it was always clear why we all had donated our time to this pursuit and loved every minute of creating a lasting project to educate future generations.

PART IV

Conclusion

Summations, Team Thoughts,
Building Performance

Ecohouse and exterior classroom

161

Students collect irrigation
water use data

162

As the need for a more environmentally
friendly way of life becomes essential
to sustaining our planet, so does an
environmental education that can create
a means to achieve it. Architecture should
provide an environment that exposes and
educates a building's occupants, even at
the youngest ages, to environmentally
sustainable principles that can be
carried and utilized throughout their
lives for the betterment of society.

After collaboration with so many people — from students to
parents to design professionals and interested community
members — Bertschi School has built the world's fourth Living
Building and the first structure to meet the Imperatives of
version 2.0 of the Challenge. The building is free of 14 Red List
chemicals and is made from regionally sourced materials. It
collects all the energy it needs each year from only the sun
and gathers all the rainwater that falls on it. Bringing the
importance of site-based solutions to the forefront, Bertschi
students are managing all the water they use within their
own site. From infiltrating unused stormwater to using
plants to clean greywater and composting all of their toilet
waste, the students are respecting the hydrologic cycle and
accounting for every drop of water they use. They grow their
food and even their art supplies. They track their water
and energy use and do all these things under the comfort
of generous supplies of daylight. But most importantly,
they are learning. They are learning the significance of
sustainable buildings and sustainable practices. They are

teaching others, inspiring others and helping to bring global attention to what is possible for the built environment.

While the structures that Bertschi School builds may be small, the impact they are making for future generations is tremendous. On many of my subsequent visits to the school since the children have been learning with their Living Building, it is clear to see, quite simply, that they get it. The students seem at home in their building, confidently interacting with net zero energy systems, the plants in the garden and the energy and water meters. They talk about the importance of their sustainable building to their classmates and bring home what they learn to their parents.

As of this writing, the Living Building is now three years old. And it is heartening to hear Brigitte Bertschi talk about her school's next challenges in helping to keep the leading sustainable concepts alive. Brigitte hopes her students continue to gain scientific knowledge about things like energy and water and understanding why it is important to make positive environmental changes. She says she hopes their time at Bertschi School "makes a lasting impact on them when they become young adults in what choices they make in their chosen field." Brigitte and so many of the faculty there work to continue to tell this story to each generation of students.

Three years after opening the doors to the new science wing, Stan notes, "our first year and a half taught us a great deal about the building and its systems as we tuned it to reach net zero energy and water. In the second eighteen-month period we have continued to measure power and water usage and strive for improvements. Through this process, the students and staff have been able to see the effects of their activities and the weather on the amount of power and water used. This has been an ongoing learning experience for everyone. For Bertschi School, that was and is the goal of constructing this building to meet the Living Building Challenge. As lifelong learners our students are receiving a solid foundation in how their activities affect their environment through the lessons learned in the Bertschi Science Wing." With the building completed, the school constantly receives great interest in it. When school ambassadors tour prospective families through the site, they often get the reaction that Tiffany characterizes as "a lot of wide eyes and gasps as they are just in awe." To her, the Living Building truly represents what is at the core of the school. "It reaffirms that it's all about the kids," says Tiffany, and that "it should always start with the kids as it did with this project — with their input on the space and it ends with their extent of learning."

This entire project was the best education for all of us on the design team. We learned the in-depth intricacies of net zero operations and the changes required to the traditional design process to accomplish this Living Building. We learned of the current state of the materials industry and the massive shift in the industry needed to provide the public with transparency and healthy materials. For the Living Building Challenge and Bertschi School, we found people willing to help, from the students to manufacturers half a world away. At a time when so many are asking "what's in it for me?" when faced with questions of sustainability, Bertschi School built what was right for everyone. They reached for the stars to grasp a level of sustainability that had never before been built — and they did it for their students.

For all of the people who had the privilege to participate in this project, we hope that the greatest legacy of Bertschi's Living Building is how it demonstrates respect for the environment and how it will serve to inspire and educate future generations.

LIVING BUILDING PARTNERS

The Bertschi School is grateful for the generous support from hundreds of donors including Bertschi families, organizations and community members who made this project possible to advance sustainability and science education for generations of students to come.

DESIGN TEAM

Geotechnical: GeoEngineers

Civil: 2020 Engineering

Landscape: GGLO

Structural: Quantum Consulting Engineers

Architectural: KMD Architects

Mechanical/Electrical/Plumbing Engineer: Rushing

Sustainability Consultant: O'Brien & Company

Contractor: Skanska USA Building, Inc.

Urban Ecologist: Back to Nature Design, LLC

Building Envelope Engineer: Morrison Hershfield

Public Relations: Parson PR

ORGANIZATIONS

Seattle Department of Planning and Development

University of Washington Integrated Design Lab

King County Green Tools

International Living Future Institute

University of Washington College of Built Environments

Cascadia Green Building Council

SUBCONTRACTORS/ DONORS

Alliance Steel Fabrication

Alpine Concrete

Ambiente European Tile Design

Brundage-Bone Concrete Pumping

Cadman

Caldwell Studio

CR Siding

Custom Interiors

Division 9

Firstline Systems

Goldfinch Brothers

G-Sky Green Walls

Hermanson Company

Hills Clark Martin and Peterson

Integrated Door Systems

Long Painting Company

Mead & Mikell

Northshore Sheetmetal

Nuprecon

Premier Building Systems

R.C. Hedreen Company

Richardson Arts

Snyder Roofing

SS Framing

Teufel Nursery

VECA Electric

Washington Hardwoods

PHOTO AND DIAGRAM CREDITS

Photography:

Derek Reeves: pages 1, 116 (left), 139 (right), 154

Kara Rue Photography: page 5

Yoram Bernet: pages 6-7, 21, 22, 23, 37, 58-59, 92-93, 135, 141

Chris Hellstern: pages 8, 10-11, 32, 49, 66 (bottom), 68, 69, 76, 77, 86, 88, 94-95, 99, 101, 104, 107 (middle & bottom), 116 (right), 117 (left), 134 (top), 129, 138 (left), 153 (left), 156, 157, 158-159

Bertschi School: pages 9, 24, 25, 26, 30-31, 38, 40, 42, 50, 54, 66 (top), 80, 84, 100 (bottom), 108-109, 118, 120, 121, 128, 130, 131, 136, 140, 142-143, 147, 152, 153 (right), 155, 162

Microsoft Corp., MDA Geospatial Services Inc.: page 19

Benjamin Benschneider: pages 28-29, 51, 52-53, 72-73, 74-75, 85, 89, 98, 110-111, 112-113, 114-115, 116 (right), 118, 120-121, 122-123, 138 (right), 139 (left), 144-145, 160-161

Stacey Smedley: page 33

ILFI: pages 34, 35

The Restorative Design Collective: page 47

GGLO: pages 56-57, 61, 150-151

Washington State Department of Natural Resources: page 60

The Nature Conservancy: pages 70, 71

West Seattle Natural Energy: pages 97, 107

Stock Exchange: pages 126 (top left & top right)

Stockvault: pages 126 (bottom left & bottom right), 133, 148-149

Graphicstock: page 134 (bottom)

Diagrams:

Heidi Bohan: pages 12, 13, 15 (top left, bottom)

Charlie Fairchild: page 20

Jason F. McLennan: page 27

Chris Hellstern: pages 43, 44, 45 (bottom), 46, 82, 83, 100 (top), 105

Stacey Smedley: page 45 (top)

Brooke Sullivan: page 63

GGLO: pages 64-65, 78, 79, 117 (right)

Sandra Noel: page 81

Envirolet: page 90

NREL: page 96

softfirm: page 102

Integrated Design Lab Seattle: page 103

INTERNATIONAL LIVING FUTURE INSTITUTE

The International Living Future Institute is an environmental NGO committed to catalyzing the transformation toward communities that are socially just, culturally rich and ecologically restorative. The Institute is premised on the belief that providing a compelling vision for the future is a fundamental requirement for reconciling humanity's relationship with the natural world. The Institute operates the Living Building Challenge, the built environment's most rigorous performance standard, and Declare, an ingredients label for building materials. It houses the Cascadia Green Building Council and Ecotone Publishing.

ECOTONE PUBLISHING

Founded by green building experts in 2004, Ecotone Publishing is dedicated to meeting the growing demand for authoritative and accessible books on sustainable design, materials selection and building techniques in North America and beyond. Located in the Cascadia region, Ecotone is well positioned to play an important part in the green design movement. Ecotone searches out and documents inspiring projects, visionary people and vital trends that are leading the design industry to transformational change toward a healthier planet.

LIVING BUILDING CHALLENGE

The Living Building Challenge is the built environment's most rigorous performance standard. It calls for the creation of building projects at all scales that operate as cleanly, beautifully and efficiently as nature's architecture. To be certified under the Challenge, projects must meet a series of ambitious performance requirements, including net zero energy, waste and water, over a minimum of 12 months of continuous occupancy.